Norton Utilities
Version 4.0
An Illustrated Tutorial

Norton Utilities
Version 4.0
An Illustrated Tutorial
Richard Evans

TAB BOOKS Inc.

Blue Ridge Summit, PA

FIRST EDITION
SECOND PRINTING

Copyright © 1988 by TAB BOOKS Inc.
Printed in the United States of America

Library of Congress Cataloging in Publication Data

Evans, Richard, 1938-
Norton Utilities version 4.0.

Includes index.
1. Norton Utilities (Computer programs)
2. Utilities (Computer programs)   I. Title.
II. Title: Norton utilities version four point
zero.
QA76.76.U84E93   1987   005.4′3   87-18276
ISBN 0-8306-2929-7 (pbk.)

Questions regarding the content of this book
should be addressed to:

Reader Inquiry Branch
TAB BOOKS Inc.
Blue Ridge Summit, PA 17294-0214

1 Peter 5:10,11

This book is dedicated to my wife Vicki, whose love and support make everything possible.

Contents

Acknowledgments

I must thank the Peter Norton organization, and specifically Mr. Brad Kingsbury, Senior Programmer, for providing advance copies and documentation for the Norton Utilities Advanced Edition and Version 4.0.

Mr. Kraig Lane, Technical Support, deserves special mention for his patience. I asked him all of the questions that appear at the end of this book, along with a few hundred more.

Introduction

THE NORTON UTILITIES ARE A GROUP OF PROGRAMS THAT PROVIDE the user with many useful tools not found on a system disk. There are also a few that perform almost the same function. These are not duplicates; they are improvements.

While the programs themselves are very useful and powerful, the documentation that accompanies them is not the easiest to understand. This causes some users to refrain from using the Utilities out of fear. Others will work their way through the booklet only far enough to learn how to use a few of the programs. Once they have a basic understanding of the program's function, they put the book down. This leaves all of them without the full benefit of the programs that they have purchased.

Throughout the industry, documentation tends to be a step-child. Programmers don't usually want to take the time to write properly. Writers usually do not know enough about the program to do the job right. This leaves the user with the choice of trying to become a programmer in order to read the programmer's notes, hoping that the documentation isn't really necessary to use the programs. I've tried to make this manual walk that narrow line between the two extremes and be both readable and useful.

PC/MS-DOS is a basic (read: "bare-bones") operating system. It provides a limited number of utilities and very little help to the user attempting to use a microcomputer to do other tasks efficiently. A good interface or means of connecting the user to his or her programs should be as transparent as possible. DOS fails this first test. When a user makes a mistake, the interface should provide a clear message that an error has been made, and some equally clear suggestions on how to correct the problem. DOS fails this test also.

The Norton Utilities cannot eliminate all of the problems and shortcomings present in DOS. But they can provide us with a number of ways to avoid contact with DOS. This will smooth over many of the DOS pitfalls. The suggestions and examples presented here have been carefully constructed to provide simple, clear, easily used bypasses. These illustrations do not pretend to be an exhaustive listing. They are presented in such a manner that the reader will be able to adapt and expand these listings into useful individual applications.

If additional support or assistance is desired, I can be found online, most evenings after 9 P.M. Eastern time. The place is DELPHI and my username is ELLISCO. Among other things, I am an assistant manager for a number of the special interest groups (SIGs). If you don't find me immediately, leave an electronic mail message. For those who don't know how to access DELPHI, a local phone call in over 600 U.S. cities, call the DELPHI Customer Service Section at 1-800-544-4005, during normal East Coast business hours, to get help. You will need a modem and communications software to take full advantage of the DELPHI system.

Why the Norton Utilities?

THE MAIN PROGRAM OF THE SET, NU (NORTON UTILITY), IS DESIGNED for data recovery ("disaster recovery" is sometimes used as an interchangeable term). There are also a number of other programs on the disks that will prove useful in the daily course of working with a microcomputer. So, before the need for the programs is imminent, relax a few minutes and get familiar with the purposes of the programs. They are well designed to do their many different tasks.

Working Copies First

The first step, as with any software distribution disk, should be to make a backup copy. This procedure will take a few minutes; while the computer does the work, continue reading.

Using freshly formatted, DS/DD disks, transfer the programs on the Norton Utility distribution disk(s) to your own disks. Do this even if you plan to install the Utilities on a hard disk. Briefly it goes like this:

1. Boot your system using PC-DOS or MS-DOS.

2. Place a Norton Utility disk in Drive A.

3. Place a blank formatted disk in Drive B.

4. Enter COPY *.* B: at the A> prompt, then press Return.

5. When copying is complete, store the original disk in a safe place. All further work will be from the copies.

To install the Utilities on a hard disk, do the following:

1. Place your Norton Utilities distribution disk in Drive A.

2. Enter C: at the A> prompt and press Return.

3. Enter MD \ NU at the C> prompt and press Return.

4. Enter CD, press the F3 key, and then press Return.

5. Enter Copy A:*.EXE or COPY A:*.COM at the C> prompt and press Return. (Version 4.0 and the Advanced Edition files use the .EXE extension; Version 3.1 and earlier files have the .COM extension.) With this technique, the unnecessary files are not copied to the hard disk.

6. Enter DEL NUDEMO.* AT THE C> and press Return. (That's "NU demo.")

7. Enter COPY A:*.HLP at the C> prompt and press Return. This step and the one before will remove the Demo program from the hard disk and add the help file program.

8. Version 4.0 and Advanced Edition users will need to replace Disk 1 of 2 with Disk 2 of 2 in Drive A. Copy NU and QU to the hard disk by entering COPY A:*.EXE at the C> prompt and then pressing Return.

9. Delete NCDEMO.EXE program by entering DEL NCDEMO.* at the C> prompt, then pressing Return.

You must verify that the SD (Speed Disk) program is fully compatible before continuing. To do this, place an expendable diskette of expendable files in Drive A. Enter SD A: at the C> prompt and press Return. One of two things will occur. Either the files on the disk will be reorganized, or an error message will display. The message will prompt you to install the ANSI.SYS driver program. In either case no harm is done to any of the files on either disk.

If the ANSI driver program is required, follow the instructions in your DOS manual or turn to the section in the next chapter on the Screen Attributes (SA) program.

10. Deleting the two demo programs may have left some small spaces between programs. To eliminate this "slack" space, run the SD program by entering SD at the C> prompt and pressing Return.

11. Now, to prevent accidental erasure of the Utilities, we are going to make them "read-only" files. Do this by entering FA /R+ at the C> prompt and pressing Return.

Users having systems with hard disks may prefer to use the original disks as their backup copies. This can be adequate for many users. Others will want to copy the programs back onto working copies of floppy disks. I would strongly recommend that hard disk users make a backup copy.

Note: Version 4.0 and the Advanced Edition have the filename extension .EXE on all files. This makes them different from the .COM filenames of your existing Version 3.0 or 3.1 Norton Utilities. This also means that the new versions will *not* overwrite the existing files.

The old version of the Norton Utilities will have to be deleted from the hard or floppy disk before copying. Failure to do this will result in there being .COM and .EXE versions of each file in the directory. The duplicated filenames will cause problems—specifically, since DOS always looks first for a .COM extension, your new versions of the Utilities will never run. Also, there is not enough space on a standard 360K DS/DD disk to hold all of the files that are in the two versions. Those with disks having a larger capacity may be able to copy two complete versions prior to seeing the "out of space" message displayed.

One of the first things I noticed was that all of the filenames were just two-letter abbreviations. I also noticed that six of the programs had longer filenames. ASK, BEEP, SHORT, LONG, WIPEDISK, and WIPEFILE are special programs. In Versions 3.0 and 3.1, the LONG command will convert the two-letter abbreviations to expanded filenames, and the SHORT command will return the expanded filenames to the two-letter abbreviations. It's your decision which filename will be displayed. If there is a README.DOC or READ.ME file on the disk you purchased, make a hard copy of the information and read it before installing the Norton Utility programs.

Version 3.1 runs on any MS/PC-DOS microcomputer with at least 128K of RAM (random access memory) and two disk drives. Almost all IBM-compatible computers, like the Texas Instrument Professional Computer, have a utility program on the system disk called EMULATE.COM. This will allow you to use the Norton Utilities.

Version 3.1 does not work in some multiuser, multitasking environments. There is no copy protection on the Utilities disks, so they may be copied to a Winchester disk or any other mass storage device.

Version 4.0 of the Norton Utilities (March 1987) or the Advanced Edition are the latest offering from Peter Norton. There are four new programs, ASK, (FI) File Info, (NI) Norton Integrator, and (NCD) Norton Change Directory. There have also been improvements in ten of the existing programs. Furthermore, there have been a few improvements which span the entire series of programs. The date stamp on your distribution disks may be newer than March 1987. There have been some minor changes in various programs since then. In the past, Peter Norton has notified registered owners by mail when new or significantly changed versions of the Utilities programs become available. Replacements and upgrades have been reasonably priced; this practice can be expected to continue.

Compatibility, Configurations, Conditions

The Norton Utilities have evolved over the years, just like computer hardware. The following information comes from the various version documents to indicate how the Norton Utilities continue to keep pace with your needs.

From Version 3.0:

128K RAM minimum, 256K RAM recommended.
One diskette drive, hard-disk compatible.
May not work on shared or network disks or with IBM's TopView.

From Version 3.1:

MS/PC-DOS 2.x required.
Fully IBM TopView compatible.

From Version 4.0:

MS/PC-DOS 2.x and 3.x compatible.
Network compatible.

From the Advanced Edition:

No changes.

Figures 1-1, 1-2, and 1-3 give directories of the three major steps in the evolution of the Norton Utilities.

Automating Computer Operations

What goes where and why? There are floppy disks, hard disks, RAM disks, and the keyboard. How do I know what I want where?

```
C:\: dir a:/w

 Volume in drive A is Norton 3.00
 Directory of   A:\

READ     ME       DEMO     BAT      BEEP     COM      DS       COM      DT       COM
FA       COM      FF       COM      FS       COM      LD       COM      LP       COM
NU       COM      SA       COM      SI       COM      TM       COM      TS       COM
VL       COM      WIPEDISK COM      WIPEFILE COM      NU       PIF      README   BAT
LONG     BAT      SHORT    BAT
        22 File(s)        30208 bytes free

C:\: dir a:/w

 Volume in drive A is Norton 3.10
 Directory of   A:\

READ     ME       DEMO     BAT      BEEP     COM      DS       COM      DT       COM
FA       COM      FF       COM      FS       COM      LD       COM      LP       COM
NU       COM      QU       COM      SA       COM      SI       COM      TM       COM
TS       COM      UD       COM      VL       COM      WIPEDISK COM      WIPEFILE COM
README   BAT      LONG     BAT      SHORT    BAT
        23 File(s)       120832 bytes free

C:\:
```

Fig. 1-1. The directory listing for Versions 3.0 and 3.1 (with the /W format used to save space).

```
C:\: dir a:/w

 Volume in drive A is NU v4.00 #1
 Directory of   A:\

READ     ME       ASK      EXE      BEEP     EXE      DS       EXE      DT       EXE
FA       EXE      FF       EXE      FI       EXE      FS       EXE      LD       EXE
LP       EXE      NCD      EXE      NI       EXE      SA       EXE      SI       EXE
TM       EXE      TS       EXE      UD       EXE      VL       EXE      WIPEDISK EXE
WIPEFILE EXE      NU       HLP      FILEINFO FI       NUDEMO   BAT      FILE1    BAT
MARY
        26 File(s)        69632 bytes free

C:\: dir a:/w

 Volume in drive A is NU v4.00 #2
 Directory of   A:\

NU       EXE      QU       EXE      NU       HLP      TUTORIAL NTS      NCDEMO   EXE
_FILE_0  DBD
         6 File(s)       146432 bytes free
```

Fig. 1-2. The directory listing for Version 4.0 (with the /W format used to save space.)

```
Volume in drive A is NU Adv Ed 1
Directory of   A:\

ASK      EXE    BEEP     EXE    DS      EXE    DT      EXE    FA      EXE
FF       EXE    FI       EXE    FR      EXE    FS      EXE    LD      EXE
LP       EXE    NCD      EXE    NI      EXE    SA      EXE    SD      EXE
SI       EXE    TM       EXE    TS      EXE    UD      EXE    VL      EXE
WIPEDISK EXE    WIPEFILE EXE    NU      HLP    FILEINFO FI    NUDEMO  BAT
FILE1    BAT    MARY            READ    ME
         28 File(s)     14336 bytes free

Volume in drive A is NU Adv Ed 2
Directory of   A:\

NU       EXE    QU       EXE    NU      HLP    NCDEMO  EXE    _FILE_0 DBD
TUTORIAL NTS
          6 File(s)     116736 bytes free
```

Why would I want to put it there and, once it's there, can I change its location? Even if every microcomputer were exactly the same. Each microcomputer user is different. Users who do similar things on their computers may prefer different ways of doing them. Some of these differences can be dictated by the machine itself, some others by differences in the software.

So where does that leave us? There are numerous choices available and each of us must consider our needs. Those things that I like and use or that Peter Norton mentions may be valueless to you. Our goals are similar. Through suggestions and examples, we would hope to provide you with the ability to construct useful assisting programs ("tools," if you like) to make maximum use of your system using the minimum amount of repeated effort.

As a user, you have one ability totally missing from the computer—the ability to think. The programs, tools, power, and speed of the computer can all be focused to provide you with the time and information necessary to think and decide. The computer, even considering the latest advances in "artificial intelligence" programming and multiprocessor hardware construction, does not think. You have the final word.

Building helpful programs using special files such as CONFIG.SYS or ASK.EXE or AUTOEXEC.BAT can make daily operations much quicker and easier. Notice the first word of the last sentence: *building*. This means that these are constructed according to a plan—your plan. Work with paper, pencil, and a large eraser before you turn your computer on. By building these programs correctly, the first time, they can become very useful and powerful tools to smooth out and speed up daily tasks.

Fig. 1-3. The directory listing listing for the Norton Utilities Advanced Edition.

Remember too that you are the author of these programs. This means that you can add, change, or delete features as your needs change. This is the beginning of understanding and using some of the "real" power of your microcomputer.

Consider the "normal" operating speed of a typical microcomputer. The clock runs about 5,000,000 cycles per second. This means that it can process tremendous amounts of data quickly—if the data is available. The keyboard is designed to transmit about 2400 bits per second to the CPU. If each letter or number is 8 bits—plus another 8 bits to store shift, Alt, and Ctrl key information—this translates to about 150 keystrokes or keystroke combinations (e.g., a capital letter) per second. Using a word length of 5 letters and a space, this equates to a theoretical typing speed of 1500 words per minute.

While this rate of input is beyond the human user, it is still extremely slow for the computer. It is looking for something in excess of 300,000 keystrokes per second. This means that the only way to approach keeping the CPU busy is to provide it with information more efficiently. Data in memory (Random Access Memory) is the most quickly available. Data on disk (a mass storage device) can be transferred to RAM quickly and efficiently. Therefore, keeping continuously needed data in RAM and frequently needed data on disk provides the more efficient way to use the speed of your machine.

DOS provides two means of helping you feed data to your computer quickly. One is the AUTOEXEC.BAT file and the other is the CONFIG.SYS file. Along with the Norton Utilities, there are some useful utilities available on the DOS disk. We will be suggesting uses for some of these as we go along. One of the MS-DOS utilities available is RAMDISK.DEV (called VDISK.SYS in the IBM version of DOS). This utility can convert a portion of your system RAM into the electronic equivalent of another disk drive (usually named with the next available letter after the last physical disk drive). Like the utility ANSI.SYS, which we will be discussing in detail a bit later, RAMDISK must be a part of the CONFIG.SYS program before booting, if it is to be available. RAM disks are faster than hard or floppy disks. They are also temporary and take up some space; this is electronic RAM space, of course, not physical space.

Your electronic space may be more limited than your physical space. The installed chips are the electronic memory space available. DOS and the contents of your CONFIG.SYS program occupy some of that electronic space. Space must be kept available for applications programs, too. This means that care must be taken to select the right number and type of RAM-resident programs to permit everything to run correctly . Filling RAM with useful tools may prevent running necessary applications.

The Norton Utilities contain some helpful programs to assist you with RAM management. There are also the utilities like SD to improve data transfer from disk to RAM. As we progress, we will try to guide ourselves toward balancing the residents of RAM with the applications being run. In this way, hopefully, we will realize the greatest benefits from microcomputer usage.

The Utilities Briefly

Here is a capsule rundown of each of the Norton Utilities:

ASK

ASK (which has no SHORT filename) is used to create interactive batch files which will simplify task management. This may be the most useful utility added to the Norton Utilities since the NU program was introduced.

BEEP

BEEP (which also has no SHORT filename) sounds a computer tone. To check it out, enter BEEP MARY at the DOS prompt, then press Return. You should hear a verse of "Mary Had a Little Lamb" played through your computer's speaker. More information and a limited number of example "tonefiles" are in the BEEP program section.

Directory Sort

DS sorts the files in directories by their name, extension, size, and date. Random reorganization is also possible using the interactive mode of DS. With this method, you can place files in any order for the directory listing. The data contained in these files is not relocated.

Disk Test

DT tests for damage on a disk. It can also make some types of repairs. Used most often with the DOS CHKDSK utility, these programs provide the best means of being able to recover data from disks that have been damaged in some way. NU may be able to complete the recovery process by rebuilding the still damaged files bit by bit.

File Attributes

FA displays/sets/changes the attributes of files. This program parallels the features available in the later versions of DOS which contain the ATTRIB utility. FA contains improvements to the DOS utility.

File Information

FI attaches to filenames descriptive comments up to 65 characters long. It also allows for editing and deleting comments. These comments are then either fully visible and readable, visible in shortened form, or invisible. Using the DOS DIR command will not display either form of the comments. This utility makes the cryptic filenames required by DOS's eight-character limitation less of an annoyance to use. Just number the files (this keeps the names unique) and uses FI to describe the contents in clear text.

Format Recovery

FR allows for recovering data on a hard disk that has accidentally been reformatted. This is possible only if the program has been run at least once before with the /SAVE switch active. FR needs the file produced by that first run in order to rebuild the hard disk. An idea or two on how to do this in a semi-automated way are shown in the section on the ASK utility.

File Find

FF searches all directories on all drives for a filename. The wildcard characters * and ? are accepted just in case the full filename isn't correctly remembered.

File Size

FS displays the actual size of the file(s) and the amount of disk space used by the file(s). FS can also indicate the amount of disk space required to copy the file(s) to a target disk. This can prevent the error message "insufficient disk space, 0 files copied" from appearing. The percentage of "slack" or empty space can also indicate that it may be time to use the SD (Speed Disk) utility.

List Directories

LD provides a listing—to the monitor, a disk file, or printer—of the selected directories.

Line Print

LP is a simple formatter routine for printing ASCII files, files containing European characters or files coded in EBCDIC (the code format of IBM mainframes). LP should not be mistaken for an editor or a word processor, however.

Norton Change Directory

NCD allows for the making, changing or deleting of directories without having to enter the entire pathname. It also displays the entire directory structure graphically. Using NCD also means that movement from directory to directory is direct, without the need to enter entire pathnames.

Norton Integrator

The NI program provides an integrated environment for using all of the Norton Utilities, including help screens and Speed Search. It is a gateway program to all of the Utilities. Used in an ASK file, it can further improve the flexibility of movement between tasks.

Norton Utilities

NU is the main program in this utility set and performs a number of services. Disk exploration and data recovery are its most notable features. Data modification using one of its editing capabilities makes many previously inaccessible code combinations easily available. Now you can redate all of your files and make them look like those professional distribution disks that come in commercial software.

Quick UnErase

QU is an abbreviated form of the UnErase feature in the NU program. It is faster to use but does not have all of the features found in the NU program. This is the first "life preserver" to reach for when trouble comes. Your other recovery tools are CHKDSK, DT, and NU. If all of these fail, professional assistance may help. Otherwise the data must be considered lost.

Screen Attributes

SA sets the foreground and/or background colors of the screen while running DOS. Some systems also require that the ANSI.SYS driver be installed before this utility will run. ANSI.SYS must be specified in another file called CONFIG.SYS, which also may contain some other very useful features that will be discussed later. Some further discussion on this DOS utility can be found in the section covering the ASK utility.

Speed Disk

SD reorganizes disk files to eliminate file fragmentation, and also generates a fragmentation report. This utility differs from many of the other "disk optimizer" programs in that it recognizes that there are certain files that should not be relocated during an optimizing session. This program thus provides two useful services. It reduces access times by placing all files into contiguous sectors and it leaves the "signature" files, written by some protected software, in place. This insures that they can be found by the primary program.

System Information

SI displays some of the technical information about your computer.

Time Mark

TM displays the current time and is also useful as a stopwatch. Task timing, either for record-keeping purposes or to check coding improvements, is one of the more common uses of TM. Look for it when you exit the NU program.

Text Search

TS is a case-in sensitive search routine which can search file(s) or directories for a specified variable.

UnRemove Directory

UD is an UnErase routine for directories. The directory had to be empty before it was deleted, unless there was an accident of some type. This fact should keep the amount of information lost to a minimum. If the deleted files within the selected directory have not been overwritten, they too are recoverable.

Volume Label

VL allows writing or changing disk labels, without having to reformat the disk. Unlike the LABEL command in later versions of DOS, the VL command permits lowercase letters.

WIPEDISK

WIPEDISK (which for safety reasons has no SHORT filename) overwrites the entire disk. It is also able to overwrite the unused portions of a disk. This feature can ensure that only the data known to be in the active files is given to someone else. By overwriting the system, directory, and data areas, WIPEDISK insures that nothing can be recovered from any portion of a disk.

WIPEFILE

WIPEFILE (no SHORT filename) overwrites a specified file. This is a true delete. Nothing is left of the file in the File Allocation Table

(FAT), directory, or data areas. This is different from the DELete command, which simply erases the first character of the file's directory entry. This indicates to DOS that the spaces in the FAT, directory, and data areas formerly occupied by the deleted file(s) are now available for reuse. If WIPEFILE has not been used, QU or NU should be able to recover the file. Only the overwritten portions, if any, will be lost.

READ.ME

The READ.ME file contains important information not found in the manual accompanying the Norton Utilities.

These are the tools available; the next chapter is a complete description of the programs and their uses. Also included are representations of the screen displays that are typical for these programs. Comments are included to clarify the display information.

All of these programs work. They will do what they claim, but they also can cause problems if they are not properly used. The WIPE programs, for example, are so thorough at removing information from a disk that after WIPEDISK is used the disk must be reformatted before reuse. Remember too, HIDDEN and SYSTEM files do not appear on the display of a directory. This can be both a boon and a bane.

Note that the filename conversion utilities SHORT.BAT and LONG.BAT are not part of the program group in Version 4.0. If you want to use long names you will have to rename the file individually. There are no LONG filenames for the new programs.

Notation Conventions

The following notation conventions are used throughout this book:

[ ]   Square brackets are used to indicate the various optional parameters to a Norton Utility filename for customized output.

>*drive/path/filename*   The DOS command to redirect the program output to a disk file. This parameter is active for most Norton Utilities programs. The exceptions are noted in the section devoted to that program. An existing file with the same filename will be overwritten by this command.

>>*filename*   The DOS command to append the program output to the end of an existing disk file. The file is created if it does not exist.

>**LPTI or PRNT**   The DOS command to redirect the program output to the system printer.

The vertical bar separating two choices indicates that the choices are mutually exclusive. This means you can use only one at a time.

For uniformity, only the two-letter filename is used in the running text and examples. The LONG filenames or the programs are shown at the tops of the opening pages of the sections devoted to each program. Since the programs added in version 4.0 and the Advanced Edition have no other name, this listing is also modified.

Keystroke Translation

For those computers that cannot use the function keys or the cursor control keys indicated throughout this book. Table 1-1 provides a listing of ANSI-equivalent key combinations. The caret symbol ^ means to

Function Key	ANSI Equivalent
F1	^O
F2	^F
F3	^G
F4	^U
F5	^J
F6	^K
F7	^L
F8	^V
F9	^B
F10	^N
Cursor Key	
Up Arrow	^E
Down Arrow	^X
Right Arrow	^S
Left Arrow	^D
PgUp	^R
PgDn	^C
Home	^W
End	^Z

Fig. 1-4. ANSI keyboard equivalences.

press the Ctrl key together with the indicated letter key. (These functions are not case-sensitive.)

These combinations are available for use in the following Norton Utility programs:

DS	(Directory Sort)
NCD	(Norton Change Directory)
NU	(Norton Utility)
SD	(Speed Disk)

AUTOEXEC.BAT and CONFIG.SYS

The Norton Utilities are written so that they are compatible with most MS-DOS machines. Where the coding requires IBM compatibility, a switch is provided to bypass this necessity. This means that the Utilities should run on virtually any DOS machine. Clones are included, as well as those only partially compatible machines like the TIPC. With this in mind let's proceed to customize our system to suit our needs.

The first executable file that DOS runs after boot-up is completed is the AUTOEXEC.BAT file. If this file is not present, the DOS prompt is displayed to indicate that the system is ready for user input. Before running the AUTOEXEC.BAT file, DOS looks for and examines a text file named CONFIG.SYS.

The CONFIG.SYS file contains information which is used by DOS to customize the operating system, to a limited degree. We both know that there is a section somewhere in your DOS manual that covers the use and contents of a CONFIG.SYS file. Rather than forcing you to dig out and dust off that manual, the following is provided as a suggestion.

```
FILES = 20
BUFFERS = 10
DEVICE = ANSI.SYS
```

Buffers are temporary data holding areas used by DOS during disk read/write operations. There is a default of 4 set when a CONFIG.SYS file is not present. These buffers are the same length as the sectors on your diskettes: 512 bytes plus 14 bytes of overhead (528 bytes). Their purpose is to store data moving to and from disk and memory. The exact number of buffers required for different applications can vary. Applications programs that do not read and write to disk often require very few buffers. Applications like database management programs may require more. A reasonable guide is between 10 and 20 for a diskette-only systems and 4 to 10 for systems with hard disks. Since buffers reserve RAM, keeping them to a reasonable minimum allows other things to occupy the remaining space.

ANSI.SYS which belongs to a class of programs known as *device drivers*, provides enhanced keyboard and screen control, and is used by some of the Norton Utilities. ANSI.SYS replaces the default CON: driver normally installed by DOS, although some computers (such as the TI Pro) automatically boot with the enhanced driver.

By default, DOS allows only eight files to be open at any one time, although it has the ability to handle as many as 99 open files. Increasing the number of files permitted to be open from 8 to 20 uses 39 bytes per allowable open file; 468 bytes of memory will be reserved when this command is in the CONFIG.SYS file. Database management programs normally require something above the default number of open files in order to run properly.

Meet the Players

NOW THAT YOU'VE SEEN THE ROSTER OF THE NORTON UTILITIES team, this chapter will let you get to know the players individually. Before doing so, however, let's look at the notational conventions one more time:

[ ]   Square brackets are used to indicate the various optional parameters to a Norton Utility command for customized output.

>*drive/path/filename*   This is the DOS command to redirect the program output to a disk file. This parameter is active for most Norton Utilities programs. The exceptions are noted in the section devoted to that program. An existing file with the same filename will be overwritten by this command.

> >*filename*   The DOS command to append the program output to the end of an existing disk file. As noted in the DOS manual, the file is created if it does not exist.

>**LPT1: or PRN:**   The DOS command to redirect the program output to the system printer.

| The vertical bar separating two choices indicates that the choices are mutually exclusive. This means you can use only one at a time.

Norton ASK

ASK is a simple program-writing feature that allows the building of interactive batch files. These batch files can contain the command strings that are used to move to the drive, directory, subdirectory, and filename of a selected application.

Format: ASK [*"prompt"*] [*key-list*]

The command-line options are:

"prompt"   The optional character string displayed when ASK runs.

key-list   An optional listing of alphanumeric response symbols. (If no *key-list* is present, any keypress is accepted.)

ASK provides the means for building a very "user friendly" interface to applications programs. This may not be one of the highest priorities for a "power user," who *never* allows his or her system to be used by anyone else, it can make life much easier for those of us who cannot afford the luxury of an "exclusive" system. Experts can help new users by installing ASK. It is much easier to explain how to use the menu than to teach a person all of the necessary DOS commands.

ASK is an improvement on the DOS batch processing capability in that ASK permits real-time interaction with a running batch file; the user is not locked into one fixed sequence of commands. This added flexibility can expand into providing a greater variety of options for task completion. The first benefit of ASK could be the integration of many small batch files into one larger, interactive ASK file. This would tend to simplify operation and would also save time and disk space.

For those who have never written a batch file, it is much like writing a macro or script in application programs. In the batch file shown

```
ASK "Run the (D)atabase, (W)ord processor, or (Q)uit?", dwq
REM     the letters "dwq" after the comma are the acceptable
REM     inputs from the keyboard. If no characters are
REM     present, any keyboard entry is acceptable
REM
  if errorlevel 3 goto quit
REM
REM     branching instructions (if/then/elseif) are placed
REM     in reverse order to the ASK listing.
REM
  if errorlevel 2 goto words
  if errorlevel 1 goto base
REM
REM     this last branch is not necessary if the database
REM     commands follow immediately, as they do here.
REM
:base
  c:\lotus\123
  goto quit
:words
  c:\wp\ewii
  goto quit
REM
REM     the last goto line is unnecessary since "quit"
REM     follows immediately.
:quit
```

Fig. 2-1. A simple menu-generating batch file using Norton ASK.

in Fig. 2-1 the REM statements are the documentation for the program file.

Using the same logic, writing a much more extensive ASK-based batch file is possible (Fig. 2-2). ECHO OFF prevents the display of unwanted information lines. CLS allows a full screen of information to be displayed before scrolling starts. A variation of this could be to have all programs return to ASK rather than quitting. Then QUIT could run HOUSEKEEPING before actually returning to the DOS prompt.

If ASK is on a floppy disk in Drive A, remember to place the drive letter as well as the path in the instructions under each choice. Also, remember to use the drive letter to return to ASK after completing the selected task.

Another possibility is to change the screen colors for different applications programs. This can be done by incorporating the SA (q.v.) command line into any or all of the code segments being used.

Some purists may consider interposing a program between them and their chips a sacrilege. For most of us, having an easy-to-read menu instead of the DOS prompt is an encouraging start. The programs

```
echo off
cls
REM   CLS follows ECHO OFF so that the  full screen is
REM   cleared. If they are reversed ECHO OFF is displayed.
echo Enter the first letter of the choice run next.
echo Programs or tasks available are:
echo
REM      An ASCII 255 character is placed on the line after
REM      the last "echo" as a spacer. To enter this
REM      character, press the ALT key and enter the numbers
REM      255 from the numeric keypad.
REM
echo (B)asic
echo (C)ommunications
echo (E)ditor, Norton
echo (G)raphics
echo (H)ousekeeping
echo (I)nfo, File
echo (L)otus
echo (M)ultiMate
echo (N)orton Utilities
echo (P)ascal
echo (S)uperCalc
echo (Q)uit
echo
REM      ASCII 255 on previous line
ASK "Your request: ", bceghilmnpsq
  if errorlevel 12 goto quit
  if errorlevel 11 goto super
        .
        .
  if errorlevel 1 goto basic
REM
:basic
  c:\bas\basic
  goto quit
:commo
  c:\comm\term
  goto quit
      .
      .
REM Just in case someone asks--
:housekeeping
  c:\nu\fr /save>a:
  goto quit
REM      this writes/overwrites the FRECOVER.DAT file on
REM      the disk in the A: drive.

      .
      .
:super
  c:\cal\sc4
REM quit returns you to the DOS prompt of the default drive.
:quit
```

Fig. 2-2. A more extensive ASK-based batch file.

provided by the Norton Utilities are not "toys" or "gadgets." They are useful tools which become more valuable as you learn more about each one of them.

Batch File Definitions

Here are the definitions of the MS-DOS batch file commands used in Figs. 2-1 and 2-2:

ECHO   Display the balance of this line on the monitor.

ECHO ON   Display everything following on the monitor.

ECHO OFF Do not display anything following on the monitor.

REM   A remark or a means of providing internal documentation. These lines may or may not display, depending on the setting of the ECHO ON/OFF switch.

How can I prevent everybody, including me, from reformatting my hard disk?

The quickest way is to eliminate the FORMAT.COM program from the DOS directory. Another way is to rename the format program.

Assume that we REName FORMAT.COM as XQWZ.COM. Then we can establish a .BAT file called FORMAT.BAT containing the single line:

    XQWZ A:

Since this is a fixed file, we would lose the /S option which formats bootable floppy disks. If a second .BAT file were called FORSYS.BAT and contained the line:

    XQWZ A:/S

the problem would be solved. Floppy disks still can be formatted, but the hard disk cannot. To reformat the hard disk, it would be necessary to boot from Drive A: using a backup copy of the DOS system disk.

Now that I've done that, how do I remember the batch file names?

They are good candidates for an ASK interactive file.

The list of options I want available exceeds a full screen. How do I resolve that problem?

An ASK file that allows you to select other ASK files might be one solution. Figure 2-3 shows an example.

The (C)ommunications selection could go directly to the single comm program you use, or another ASK menu program could let you select the program for the occasion. Now that we have all of this laid out, how does it code? Without consuming too much space in details, the first ASK program file and a portion of the ASK utilities files are shown in Fig. 2-4. These are source code files and may be used "as is" only if everything else is the same. Check the pathnames and filenames before attempting to use them.

Note that all of the selections "quit" or exit to DOS after running just one application program. It is possible to cause the system to "loop" back into one of the ASK menu programs by changing the "goto quit" line to "ASK main" or any of the other ASK menus.

```
ASK (main)                    ASK (D)atabases

    (A)pplications                (1)23
    (C)ommunications              (D)base
    (D)atabases                   (E)asyWriter
    (U)tilities                   (F)ramework
    (Q)uit                        (M)ultimate
                                  (P)aradox
                                  (R)eturn to main
ASK (A)pplications                (S)ymphony
                                  s(U)perCalc
    (A)da                         (Q)uit
    (B)asic
    (C) "C"
    (D)base                   ASK (U)tilities
    (F)ortran
    (G)raphics                    (B)ackup
    (L)isp                        (D)os
    (M)asm                        (E)ditor, Norton
    c(O)bol                       (F)ormat a floppy
    (P)rolog                      (N)orton Utilities
    (R)eturn to main              f(O)rmat a bootable floppy
    (S)nobol4+                    (R)eturn to main
    (T)urbo Pascal                (T)ape backup
    (Q)uit                        (Q)uit
```

Fig. 2-3. Example of an extensive menu structure using nested ASK-based batch files.

```
echo off
cls
REM   ASK Main Batch File
echo The following selections are available
echo (255)
echo (A)pplications
echo (C)ommunications
echo (D)atabases
echo (U)tilities
echo (Q)uit
echo (255)
ASK "Your choice: ",aceuq
    if errorlevel 5 goto quit
    if errorlevel 4 goto util
    if errorlevel 3 goto data
    if errorlevel 2 goto comm
:appl
    ASK appl
    goto quit
:comm
    ASK  comm
    goto quit
:data
    ASK data
    goto quit
:util
    ASK util
:quit
```

Fig. 2-4. Main batch file to implement the structure shown in Fig. 2-3.

If looping menus are going to be used, just remember to leave an exit somewhere. All of the Norton Utilities have an exit. This will return control to the ASK program, so don't depend on those for your only exits.

How can I know that the character after an "echo off" is 255d?

Follow the screens shown in the next six illustrations and look at what has been written to the file.

Figure 2-5 is the first screen or main menu of the NU program. It is our gateway to everything on a disk. What we want to do is look at the actual characters that have been written to the disk when we created the ASK file. To do this we will select the Explore Disk option. The reverse video block is already there so it is only necessary to press the Return key.

The Menu 1 (Explore Disk) menu assumes that we will want to select a specific item to explore (Fig. 2-6). The reverse video is again

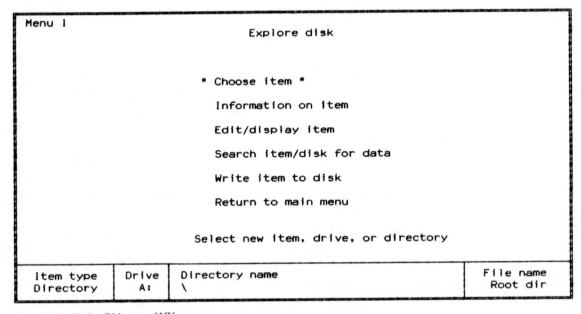

```
┌─────────────────────────────────────────────────────────────────────┐
║  The Norton Utilities  Advanced Edition  (C) Copr 1987, Peter Norton  ║
║              ─────────────────────────────────────────               ║
║              8:31 am, Tuesday, Month 7, 1987                          ║
╠═══════════════════════════════════════════════════════════════════════╣
║                          Main menu                                    ║
║                                                                       ║
║                   * Explore disk *                                    ║
║                                                                       ║
║                   UnErase                                             ║
║                                                                       ║
║                   Disk information                                    ║
║                                                                       ║
║                   Quit the Norton Utilities                           ║
║                                                                       ║
║                                                                       ║
║              View, edit, search, or copy selected item                ║
║                                                                       ║
╠──────────────┬──────┬─────────────────────────────┬──────────────────╣
║  Item type   │Drive │ Directory name              │    File name     ║
║  Directory   │A:    │ \                           │    Root dir      ║
└──────────────┴──────┴─────────────────────────────┴──────────────────┘
```

Fig. 2-5. Main menu of the NU program.

```
┌─────────────────────────────────────────────────────────────────────┐
║ Menu 1                                                                ║
║                            Explore disk                               ║
║                                                                       ║
║                                                                       ║
║                   * Choose item *                                     ║
║                                                                       ║
║                   Information on item                                 ║
║                                                                       ║
║                   Edit/display item                                   ║
║                                                                       ║
║                   Search item/disk for data                          ║
║                                                                       ║
║                   Write item to disk                                  ║
║                                                                       ║
║                   Return to main menu                                 ║
║                                                                       ║
║              Select new item, drive, or directory                    ║
║                                                                       ║
╠──────────────┬──────┬─────────────────────────────┬──────────────────╣
║  Item type   │Drive │ Directory name              │    File name     ║
║  Directory   │A:    │ \                           │    Root dir      ║
└──────────────┴──────┴─────────────────────────────┴──────────────────┘
```

Fig. 2-6. The Explore Disk menu of NU.

over the item we are interested in. Pressing Return again takes us
to Menu 1.1 (Fig. 2-7) which defaults to the File selection.

Another press of the Return key displays Menu 1.1.3, which is
the file or subdirectory menu (Fig. 2-8). Since the ASK code file is
on a floppy disk, there are only a few files and no subdirectories. Pressing

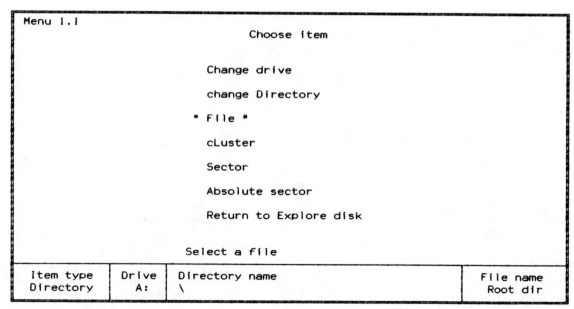

```
Menu 1.1
                              Choose Item


                        Change drive

                        change Directory

                      * File *

                        cLuster

                        Sector

                        Absolute sector

                        Return to Explore disk


                    Select a file
```

Item type Directory	Drive A:	Directory name \	File name Root dir

Fig. 2-7. The Choose Item menu of NU.

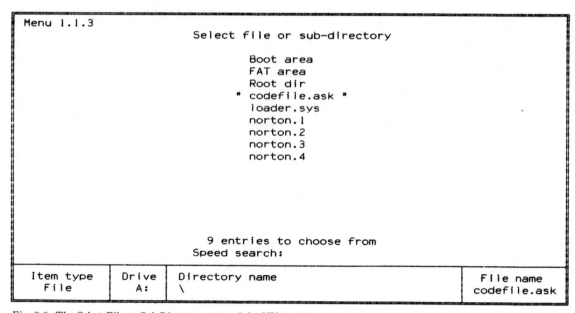

```
Menu 1.1.3
                        Select file or sub-directory

                            Boot area
                            FAT area
                            Root dir
                          * codefile.ask *
                            loader.sys
                            norton.1
                            norton.2
                            norton.3
                            norton.4










                    9 entries to choose from
                    Speed search:
```

Item type File	Drive A:	Directory name \	File name codefile.ask

Fig. 2-8. The Select File or Sub-Directory menu of the NU program.

Return after positioning the reverse video over the filename
CODEFILE.ASK returns us to Menu 1.

Now we want to Edit/Display the data in file CODEFILE.ASK.
Pressing the "E" key takes us directly to the beginning of that file
(Fig. 2-9). Along the top edge of the screen window are the filename

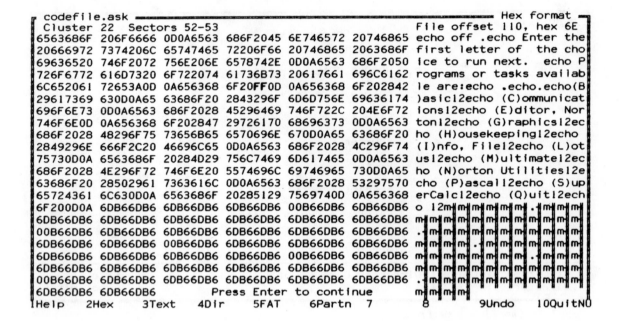

```
 codefile.ask ═══════════════════════════════════ Hex format ═
  Cluster 22  Sectors 52-53                  File offset 110, hex 6E
6563686F  206F6666  0D0A6563  686F2045  6E746572  20746865  echo off .echo Enter the
20666972  7374206C  65747465  72206F66  20746865  2063686F  first letter of  the cho
69636520  746F2072  756E206E  6578742E  0D0A6563  686F2050  ice to run next.  echo P
726F6772  616D7320  6F722074  61736B73  20617661  696C6162  rograms or tasks availab
6C652061  72653A0D  0A656368  6F20FF0D  0A656368  6F202842  le are:echo .echo.echo(B
29617369  630D0A65  63686F20  2843296F  6D6D756E  69636174  )asicl2echo (C)ommunicat
696F6E73  0D0A6563  686F2028  45296469  746F722C  204E6F72  ionsl2echo (E)ditor, Nor
746F6E0D  0A656368  6F202847  29726170  68696373  0D0A6563  tonl2echo (G)raphicsl2ec
686F2028  48296F75  73656B65  6570696E  670D0A65  63686F20  ho (H)ousekeepingl2echo
2849296E  666F2C20  46696C65  0D0A6563  686F2028  4C296F74  (I)nfo, Filel2echo (L)ot
75730D0A  6563686F  20284D29  756C7469  6D617465  0D0A6563  usl2echo (M)ultimatel2ec
686F2028  4E29726F  746F6E20  5574696C  69746965  730D0A65  ho (N)orton Utilitiesl2e
63686F20  28502961  7363616C  0D0A6563  686F2028  53297570  cho (P)ascall2echo (S)up
65724361  6C630D0A  6563686F  20285129  7569740D  0A656368  erCalcl2echo (Q)uitl2ech
6F200D0A  6DB66DB6  6DB66DB6  6DB66DB6  00B66DB6  6DB66DB6  o l2m m m m m m .m m m
6DB66DB6  6DB66DB6  6DB66DB6  6DB66DB6  6DB66DB6  6DB66DB6  m m m m m m m m m m m m
00B66DB6  6DB66DB6  6DB66DB6  6DB66DB6  6DB66DB6  6DB66DB6  .m m m m m m m m m m m
6DB66DB6  6DB66DB6  00B66DB6  6DB66DB6  6DB66DB6  6DB66DB6  m m m m m .m m m m m m
6DB66DB6  6DB66DB6  6DB66DB6  6DB66DB6  00B66DB6  6DB66DB6  m m m m m m .m m m m m
6DB66DB6  6DB66DB6  6DB66DB6  6DB66DB6  6DB66DB6  6DB66DB6  m m m m m m m m m m m m
00B66DB6  6DB66DB6  6DB66DB6  6DB66DB6  6DB66DB6  6DB66DB6  .m m m m m m m m m m m
6DB66DB6  6DB66DB6          Press Enter to continue        m m m m
1Help   2Hex    3Text    4Dir    5FAT    6Partn   7        8        9Undo   10QuitNU
```

and the format being used to display this sector. By pressing the F3 key we can change the format into something more readable to us (Fig. 2-10).

In this format, we can easily locate the characters we are interested in. They are the dots or periods after each of the "echo" commands on the lines by themselves. However, we cannot tell what those character values are in this format. Pressing the F2 key returns us to the Hex format (Fig. 2-9). Pressing the Tab key once moves the blinking cursor to the text half of the screen. Then, using the arrow keys, we can place the blinking cursor over the dot after the last "echo." Can't find the dot? Maybe you made the mistake I made: I didn't enter the ASCII character value 255 after the second "echo." Look again at the information displayed in Fig. 2-9. The 15th line, first block, reads F6200D0A. This is much different than the 5th line, 3rd block, which reads 6F20FF0D. The 0A begins the next block. When the Tab key was pressed, the cursor on left half of the screen went from a blinking block over one letter to a solid reverse video block over two letters. It's possible to edit the data in either form. Just remember that it is the data under the blinking cursor block that is being changed. Some data can be edited only in the Hex portion of the screen; 0Dh (Carriage Return) and 0Ah (Line Feed) are two of those characters.

You will note, in fact, that these characters have been changed completely in the screen dumps. They caused the printer to perform those actions when the computer dumped them.

Fig. 2-9. Hexadecimal display of the batch file shown in Fig. 2-4. (Note the boldface FF and period on the fifth line of the dump. Note also that the carriage return and line feed characters 0Dh and 0Ah are represented by the numerals 1 and 2 in the ASCII portion of the display; this was done to allow proper printing of the screen.)

```
codefile.ask ══════════════════════════════════════════ Text format ═
  Cluster 22  Sectors 52-53                       File offset 0, hex 00

  echo off
  echo Enter the first letter of the choice to run next.
  echo Programs or tasks available are:
  echo .
  echo (B)asic
  echo (C)ommunications
  echo (E)ditor, Norton
  echo (G)raphics
  echo (H)ousekeeping
  echo (I)nfo, File
  echo (L)otus
  echo (M)ultimate
  echo (N)orton Utilities
  echo (P)ascal
  echo (S)uperCalc
  echo (Q)uit
  echo
  m6m6m6m6m6m6.m6m6m6m6m6m6m6m6m6m6m6m6m6m6.m6m6m6m6m6m6m6m6m6m6m6m6m6m
    6.m6m6m6m6m6m6m6m6m6m6m6m6m6m6m6m6m6.m6m6m6m6m6m6m6m6m6m6m6m6m6m6.m6m6m6m6m
    6...more
                       Press Enter to continue
Help  ═2Hex   ═3Text  ═4Dir   ═5FAT   ═6Partn ═7      ═8      ═9Undo  ═10QuitNU
```

Fig. 2-10. Text display of the batch
file listed in Fig. 2-4. Note the boldface
ECHO commands.

The sequence of characters and Hex values at the end of the first "echo" are:

o . 1 2   (in text)
6F 20 FF 0D 0A   (in HEX)

The character represented by 1 above normally displays on the screen as a musical note, and 2 normally displays as a reverse video block with a diamond centered in it. You can verify these values by moving the cursor with the arrow keys. Set the blinking cursor to the right side so that the solid block highlights the two Hex values that make up that character. Try making some changes. Toggle between the F2 Hex format (Fig. 2-11) and the F3 Text format (Fig. 2-12). Notice, too, that all of the characters that have been changed are either bold or in yellow.

There are two possibilities when you finish. You can either cancel the changes by pressing the F9 key or, press Esc to leave. Pressing Return will take you to the last portion of the file, which is in the next sector.

If you have not canceled the changes, pressing Esc or Return will have the same effect. You will see Menu 1.3 (Fig. 2-13). This menu gives you three choices. Save the changes, discard them, or return to the previous screen to review them. If you're not sure that what you have done is correct, either review or discard. Once you are positive of the changes, tell NU to write them into the file.

```
┌ codefile.ask ━━━━━━━━━━━━━━━━━━━━━━━━━━━━━━━━━━━━━━━ Hex format ━┐
│  Cluster 22   Sectors 52-53                    File offset 338, hex 0152│
│ 6563686F  206F6666  0D0A6563  686F2045  6E746572  20746865  echo off12echo Enter the│
│ 20666972  7374206C  65747465  72206F66  20746865  2063686F   first letter of the cho│
│ 69636520  746F2072  756E206E  6578742E  0D0A6563  686F2050  ice to run next.12echo P│
│ 726F6772  616D7320  6F722074  61736B73  20617661  696C6162  rograms or tasks availab│
│ 6C652061  72653A0D  0A656368  6F20FF0D  0A656368  6F202842  le are:12echo .12echo (B│
│ 29617369  630D0A65  63686F20  2843296F  6D6D756E  69636174  )asic12echo (C)ommunicat│
│ 696F6E73  0D0A6563  686F2028  45296469  746F722C  204E6F72  ions12echo (E)ditor, Nor│
│ 746F6E0D  0A656368  6F202847  29726170  68696373  0D0A6563  ton12echo (G)raphics12ec│
│ 686F2028  48296F75  73656B65  6570696E  670D0A65  63686F20  ho (H)ousekeeping12echo │
│ 2849296E  666F2C20  46696C65  0D0A6563  686F2028  4C29746F  (I)nfo, File12echo (L)ot│
│ 75730D0A  6563686F  20284D29  756C7469  6D617465  0D0A6563  us12echo (M)ultimate12ec│
│ 686F2028  4E29726F  746F6E20  5574696C  69746965  730D0A65  ho (N)orton Utilities12e│
│ 63686F20  28502961  7363616C  0D0A6563  686F2028  53297570  cho (P)ascal12echo (S)up│
│ 65724361  6C630D0A  6563686F  20285129  7569740D  0A656368  erCalc12echo (Q)uit12ech│
│ 6F20FF0D  0AB66DB6  6DB66DB6  6DB66DB6  00B66DB6  6DB66DB6  o .12▌m▌m▌m▌m▌m▌.▌m▌m▌m▌m│
│ 6DB66DB6  6DB66DB6  6DB66DB6  6DB66DB6  6DB66DB6  6DB66DB6  m▌m▌m▌m▌m▌m▌m▌m▌m▌m▌m▌m│
│ 00B66DB6  6DB66DB6  6DB66DB6  6DB66DB6  6DB66DB6  6DB66DB6  .▌m▌m▌m▌m▌m▌.▌m▌m▌m▌m▌m│
│ 6DB66DB6  6DB66DB6  00B66DB6  6DB66DB6  6DB66DB6  6DB66DB6  m▌m▌m▌m▌.▌m▌m▌m▌m▌m▌m▌m│
│ 6DB66DB6  6DB66DB6  6DB66DB6  6DB66DB6  00B66DB6  6DB66DB6  m▌m▌m▌m▌m▌m▌.▌m▌m▌m▌m▌m│
│ 6DB66DB6  6DB66DB6  6DB66DB6  6DB66DB6  6DB66DB6  6DB66DB6  m▌m▌m▌m▌m▌m▌m▌m▌m▌m▌m▌m│
│ 00B66DB6  6DB66DB6  6DB66DB6  6DB66DB6  6DB66DB6  6DB66DB6  .▌m▌m▌m▌m▌m▌m▌m▌m▌m▌m▌m│
│ 6DB66DB6  6DB66DB6             Press Enter to continue     m▌m▌m▌m│
│Help  =2Hex   =3Text  =4Dir   =5FAT   =6Partn =7      =8      =9Undo  =10QuitN0│
└─────────────────────────────────────────────────────────────────┘
```

Fig. 2-11. Modified hexadecimal display of the Fig. 2-4 batch file. Now there are two ASCII characters with a value of 255, or FF in hex. (As in Fig. 2-9, the 0D-0A combination is displayed on the right as "12".)

```
┌ codefile.ask ━━━━━━━━━━━━━━━━━━━━━━━━━━━━━━━━━━━━━━━ Text format ━┐
│  Cluster 22   Sectors 52-53                     File offset 0, hex 00│
│                                                                  │
│   echo off                                                       │
│   echo Enter the first letter of the choice to run next.         │
│   echo Programs or tasks available are:                          │
│   echo .                                                         │
│   echo (B)asic                                                   │
│   echo (C)ommunications                                          │
│   echo (E)ditor, Norton                                          │
│   echo (G)raphics                                                │
│   echo (H)ousekeeping                                            │
│   echo (I)nfo, File                                              │
│   echo (L)otus                                                   │
│   echo (M)ultimate                                               │
│   echo (N)orton Utilities                                        │
│   echo (P)ascal                                                  │
│   echo (S)uperCalc                                               │
│   echo (Q)uit                                                    │
│   echo .                                                         │
│   m6m6m6m6m6m6.m6m6m6m6m6m6m6m6m6m6m6m6.m6m6m6m6m6m6m6m6m6m6m6.m6m6m6m6m│
│    6.m6m6m6m6m6m6m6m6m6m6m6.m6m6m6m6m6m6m6m6m6m6m6m6.m6m6m6m6m│
│    6...more                                                      │
│                         Press Enter to continue                  │
│Help  =2Hex   =3Text  =4Dir   =5FAT   =6Partn =7      =8      =9Undo  =10QuitN0│
└─────────────────────────────────────────────────────────────────┘
```

Fig. 2-12. Modified Text-format display of the file.

```
┌────────────────────────────────────────────────────────────────────┐
│  Menu 1.3                                                            │
│                    Save or discard changes made to data             │
│                                                                      │
│                                                                      │
│                                                                      │
│              You have made changes to the cluster in memory          │
│                                                                      │
│               (Changes are made and shown highlighted when           │
│                data is displayed in the hexadecimal format)          │
│                                                                      │
│                                                                      │
│                                                                      │
│                      * Write the changed data *                      │
│                                                                      │
│                        Review the changed data                       │
│                                                                      │
│                        Discard the changes                           │
│                                                                      │
│                                                                      │
│                      Write the changes to disk                       │
│                                                                      │
└────────────────────────────────────────────────────────────────────┘
```

Fig. 2-13. The Save or Discard menu of NU. On the computer screen, the first selection would be in reverse video.

BEEP

Version 3.x Directory Name   **BEEP.COM**
Version 4.0/AE Directory Name   **BEEP.EXE**

BEEP sounds a tone, a series of tones, or plays a tune (IBM or 100-percent compatibles only). For computers that are not fully compatible, BEEP will sound th standard tone once or many times; the frequency and duration switches do not operate.

Format: BEEP [*switches/drive/path/filename*]

The available switches are as follows:

/DN   The duration in $\frac{1}{18}$ of a second that the tone sounds.

/FN   The frequency (Hertz of cycles per second) of the tone.

/RN   The repetitions or number of times the tone should be sounded.

/WN   A wait or pause in $\frac{1}{18}$ of a second between tones.

drive/path/filename   This is a "tonefile" where the parameters of a tune, or other tone sequence to be played when called by BEEP. The filename may be any DOS-compatible filename; an extension is not required. The tonefile need not be on the same drive with BEEP.

When BEEP runs without parameters, the standard tone is sounded once. Adding switch parameters to the command line calling BEEP will change the tone(s) sounded. Providing a complete drive, path, and filename to BEEP runs the tune or tone sequence in the tonefile. Wildcard characters cannot be used.

Redirection of BEEP is not allowed. Having the printer attempt to act like a speaker could be disastrous. You can print tonefiles using standard DOS commands.

The $\frac{1}{18}$ second timing is based on the "tick" rate of the IBM PC's *clock interrupt*, which actually ticks 18.2 times per second. This may seem like an odd value, but it works out to 65,535 ticks per hour, the largest unsigned integer that can be represented by one "word" in a 16-bit computer. (It should be noted that the clock interrupt rate is independent of the computer's *clock frequency*, which can range from 4.77 MHz to 20 MHz or more.)

Humans normally can hear tones between 20 Hz and 20 kHz. Some lower frequency tones can also be "felt." Above 20 kHz, the tones can be heard better by some animals. They may react when a human cannot even hear the tone being generated. For reference, the A above middle C on a piano is 440 Hz.

You can write tonefiles using any ASCII editor. The tonefile segment listed in Fig. 2-14 is the first six lines of the file MARY found on the distribution disk. Note that the / (slash) is optional in a tonefile, but it is *not* optional when specifying switch parameters on the command line.

More than one set of tone parameters may be entered on a line. MARY was written in one-tone lines to match the words. Your tune choices may require other arrangements. For all "not fully compatible" computers, only the /R switch is operational. This reduces the flexibility of BEEP but it does not eliminate it as a useful utility.

Some possible uses for tonefiles are:

☐ As progress indicators during the processing of batch files.
☐ As error or event indicators.
☐ As novelty to enliven a demonstration.

```
/F330 /D2              ; Mar-
/F294 /D2              ; -y
/F262 /D2              ; had
/F294 /D2              ; a
/R2 /F330 /D2          ; little
/F330 /D4              ; lamb
;
; put a semicolon before comments
; either on a separate line
; or after the switch listing as shown above.
;
; Programmers are not accountable for their spelling.
; There is/was an error in line 28 of this file.
; Mary's,lamb had a "fleet" as white as snow.
;
```

Fig. 2-14. The first six lines of the BEEP tonefile MARY, found on the distribution disk.

How can I make my own tonefile(s)?

Use your favorite editor to create an ASCII file and then "go for it." Name the tonefile something descriptive, without an extension, and then create the file. The following two lines are equal. That is, they will be read by BEEP exactly the same.

    /F300 /D18 /R2 /W36 ; 300 Hz for 1 sec, pause for f300 d18 r2
    w36 ; 2 sec, 300 Hz for 1 sec.

The slash (/) is only required when the commands are issued on the same line that starts BEEP; within a tonefile they are not required. The semicolon separates the comments from the code.

Great, but how do I translate my sheet music into tonefile frequencies?

A translation table which gives the note names and their associated frequency is required. Be sure that the tunes are simple. The computer plays only one tone at a time. Almost any good book on the subject of acoustics in the public library will have a table.

Directory Sort

SHORT Directory Name	**DS.COM**
LONG Directory Name	**DIRSORT.COM**
Version 4.0 Directory Name	**DS.EXE**

The DS utility sorts the files in directories and subdirectories by one or a combination of parameters. For reverse order sorting use the minus sign (–) immediately after the parameter or switch. When using the minus sign and/or more than one sort parameter, do not use any spaces or punctuation between characters.

Format: DS [*sort-keys*] [*directory-name*] [/S] (for automatic sort)

DS [*directory-name*] (for full-screen interactive sort)

In automatic mode, DS writes a simple message to the screen; you must then use the DIR command to view the sorted directory:

C: \ : c: \ nu \ ds nes a:
DS-Directory Sort, Advanced Edition, (C) Copr 1987, Peter Norton

A: \ ...reading, sorting, writing, done.

C: \ :

Interactive mode, however, produces a screen such as Fig. 2-15. In both modes, the possible values for *sort-keys* are:

D Sorts files by date, oldest to newest.

E Sorts files by extension, none to .ZZZ.

N Sorts files by name, A to Z.

S Sorts files by size, smallest to largest.

T Sorts files by time stamp, 00:01 A.M. to 11:59 P.M.

– Reverses the sort order indicated above.

/S Includes all subdirectories in the sort process. This switch is only active (available) during automatic sorts.

```
C:\: c:\nu\ds a:
```

```
====================== Directory Sort ======================
┌──────────────────────── A:\ ──────────────────────────────┐
│    Name        │  Size   │    Date    │    Time    │  Sort by          Order
│  aids    txt   │ 55,102  │ Jul  5 87  │  9:39 pm   │
│  arc     doc   │ 57,214  │ Jan 12 87  │  5:06 pm   │
│  arc     exe   │ 32,184  │ Apr 22 87  │  3:08 pm   │
│  arc     txt   │  2,109  │ Apr 22 87  │  4:28 pm   │
│  arc521  com   │ 58,368  │ Jun 27 87  │  1:47 am   │
│  arce    com   │  5,710  │ Dec 31 86  │  1:54 pm   │
│  art           │  2,328  │ Jun 20 87  │  6:16 pm   │
│  ca      for   │  1,643  │ Aug  7 87  │  4:32 pm   │
│  changes 521   │  1,939  │ May 14 87  │  8:39 am   │  ──────────────────────
│  ed      for   │  1,632  │ Aug  7 87  │  4:07 pm   │
│  host          │  5,504  │ Jun 16 87  │ 10:56 pm   │        Name
│  packman arc   │ 11,136  │ Jul 10 87  │ 12:29 pm   │        Extension
│  peposcrn asm  │  5,284  │ Jun 18 87  │ 10:24 pm   │        Date
│  submit  fil   │  3,034  │ Jul  5 87  │  6:47 pm   │        Time
│  sug     for   │  1,891  │ Jan  1 80  │ 12:23 am   │        Size
│  term    log   │    592  │ Jul 14 87  │ 11:38 pm   │
│  term    sav   │      0  │ Jul  8 87  │  6:00 pm   │    Clear sort order
│                                                    │    Move sort entry
│       Space bar selects files for moving
│
│  Re-sort      Move file(s)     Change sort order     Write changes to disk
└────────────────────────────────────────────────────────────┘
```

Note: Unlike some of the other programs, DS does not use the slash (/) as a separator between the switches. It also requires no other punctuation or spaces between the switches. Only the /S switch uses the slash.

DS must not be used when other files in the directory(ies) may be used by other programs. This means that DS must be the only program running on a multiuser or multitasking system.

Because DS actually writes to the directory area of a disk, the process should be completed without attempting to abort it by using the Ctrl-Break key combination or turning the power off. Only in Version 4.0 or the Advanced Edition is it possible to abort the program using Ctrl-Break or Ctrl-C.

DS will place all subdirectories before the files in the directory, but it will not move any hidden or system files' data; this is done to prevent causing problems with copy-protected software, and with files such as IBMBIO.COM and IBMDOS.COM, whose data and directory entries must be at specific disk locations.

Version 4.0 and the Advanced Edition have an interactive mode which allows the totally arbitrary ordering of files within a directory. Entering DS without any parameters or switches will begin the interactive sort session in the default directory. The following command keys will be in effect:

Fig. 2-15. The interactive screen of the Directory Sort utility.

D	Set date as a sort parameter.
Down Arrow **PgDn**	Move the reverse video block down the list of files.
Enter	Fix the file in its new location.
Esc	Return a moved file to its original location, or leave DS and return to the DOS prompt.
F10	Exit DS and return to the DOS prompt.
Left Arrow	Shift the reverse video block from the filename listing section to the sort order section.
M	Indicates that the file highlighted by the reverse video block is to be moved.
R	Resorts the directory based on the changed parameter switches.
Tab	Acts as a toggle to move the reverse video block between the two areas.
Up Arrow **PgUp**	Moves the reverse video block up the filename listing.

Is there any "really" good reason to sort a directory?

For me, yes. I don't always remember filenames. By putting the program (.EXE or .COM) files at the beginning, I can let them scroll off the screen; the files I've created (.DAT, .TXT, or .SPT) are at the end of the listing—still visible when the prompt returns.

Can't I use the /W switch with the DIR command and see just as much?

Almost, the /W will display the filenames and extensions five to a line. Not displayed are the file size, time, and date stamp information. It's a matter of choice and/or need. This also means that different versions of a filename might appear as duplicate entries.

Can you prove that DS will not cause me problems with the "signature" files of copy-protected software on my hard disk?

Yes and no. While DS will relocate the filenames in the directory, it does not move the data portions of the files. This means that the

Filename	Ext	Size	Date	Time		Cluster	Arc	R/O	Sys	Hid	Dir	Vol
LOADER	SYS	1024	12/10/84	11:00	am	2	Arc	R/O	Sys	Hid		
INSTR	KZI	676	2/19/87	12:37	am	3	Arc					
SMSG		604	2/21/87	8:04	pm	4	Arc					
TERM	SAV		3/14/87	12:01	am							
TELE	SAV	4854	3/13/87	11:39	pm	5	Arc					
FRIED	SAV	7449	3/14/87	12:34	pm	10	Arc					
PROWARE	ARC	88960	3/14/87	1:35	pm	18	Arc					
SYSOPMAS		34304	4/01/87	12:00	am	105	Arc					
SYSOP	HAN	32278	3/30/87	9:19	pm	139	Arc					
CURSOR	COM	21524	3/09/87	12:00	am	171	Arc					
DATER	COM	21353	3/09/87	12:00	am	193	Arc					
MENU	COM	32302	3/09/87	12:00	am	214	Arc					
CURSOR	PAS	40960	3/09/87	12:00	am	246	Arc					
DATER	PAS	23552	3/09/87	12:00	am	286	Arc					
σPL	ARC	32768	3/31/87	7:03	pm	309	Arc					
σSPL	ARC		3/31/87	7:08	pm		Arc					

Filenames beginning with 'σ' indicate erased entries
Press Enter to continue

1Help 2Hex 3Text 4Dir 5FAT 6Partn 7 8 9Undo 10QuitNU

Fig. 2-16. An unsorted root directory as displayed by NU.

Filename	Ext	Size	Date	Time		Cluster	Arc	R/O	Sys	Hid	Dir	Vol
LOADER	SYS	1024	12/10/84	11:00	am	2	Arc	R/O	Sys	Hid		
CURSOR	COM	21524	3/09/87	12:00	am	171	Arc					
CURSOR	PAS	40960	3/09/87	12:00	am	246	Arc					
DATER	COM	21353	3/09/87	12:00	am	193	Arc					
DATER	PAS	23552	3/09/87	12:00	am	286	Arc					
DDS	SCR	2051	7/17/87	10:24	am	309	Arc					
FRIED	SAV	7449	3/14/87	12:34	pm	10	Arc					
INSTR	KZI	676	2/19/87	12:37	am	3	Arc					
MENU	COM	32302	3/09/87	12:00	am	214	Arc					
PROWARE	ARC	88960	3/14/87	1:35	pm	18	Arc					
SMSG		604	2/21/87	8:04	pm	4	Arc					
SYSOP	HAN	32278	3/30/87	9:19	pm	139	Arc					
SYSOPMAS		34304	4/01/87	12:00	am	105	Arc					
TELE	SAV	4854	3/13/87	11:39	pm	5	Arc					
TERM	SAV		3/14/87	12:01	am							
σSPL	ARC		3/31/87	7:08	pm		Arc					

Filenames beginning with 'σ' indicate erased entries
Press Enter to continue

1Help 2Hex 3Text 4Dir 5FAT 6Partn 7 8 9Undo 10QuitNU

Fig. 2-17. NU display of a root directory after sorting.

address (cylinder, side, and cluster/sector) of that file remain unchanged.
This should prevent problems. I've used NU to look at the root directory
of a floppy disk before and after a DS N sort (Fig. 2-16 and Fig. 2-17).
Note that the starting cluster numbers for each file are unchanged.

Will the starting cluster numbers remain unchanged if I copy the sorted files?

They will if you use the DISKCOPY utility program. Using the DOS COPY command will transfer the filenames and data areas in sorted order. This means that the starting cluster number will change and that fragmented files will be reconnected.

Isn't this almost the same as using the SD (Speed Disk) utility?

No, SD does not change the starting cluster number to suit the directory sort order. COPY is the only way to reorder the data storage area.

Doesn't this duplicate the abilities of the DOS utilities?

I don't think so. I much prefer to use SD on the hard disk as part of my routine maintenance. Using DS, then copying the files to a floppy or another portion of the hard disk, seems very time-consuming. I do sort and COPY files before sending a floppy disk to someone. I think that it looks more professional. I also use a new disk or one on which I've used WipeDisk. So there will not be any "other" data on the disk.

Disk Test

SHORT Directory Name	**DT.COM**
LONG Directory Name	**DISKTEST.COM**
Version 4.0 Directory Name	**DT.EXE**

This program tests a disk for damage, and it can repair some types of damage. Unmarked "bad" sectors on the disk are shown and, at your option, marked as unusable.

Format: DT [*d:*] [*path/filename*] [*switches*] [>|>>]
[*path/filename¦device*]

The following command-line parameters can be used:

d: Tells DT which drive contains the disk under test.

path/filename Tells DT which file, or file type (e.g., *.COM) is under test.

>|>> The DOS operators to redirect or redirect-and-append the output. There is no display when either of these operators is used.

path/filename¦device The output disk file or the printer.
The following switches are available:

/F Test each **F**ile on the disk selected.

/D(isk) Test the entire **D**isk: boot, FAT, directory, and data areas.

/B(oth) Test everything. This combines **B**oth of the tests listed above.

/LOG Adapts the program's running output into a form which is sent to the printer or a disk file. This means that only the final results are displayed/printed/filed. (New in Version 3.1.)

/Cn Mark cluster *n* as bad. This command is repeated as necessary. (New in Version 4.0.)

/Cn –	Mark cluster *n* as good. This command is repeated as necessary. (New in Version 4.0.)
/M	Move data in questionable clusters to a safe location and mark the questionable clusters as bad.
/S	Test files in subdirectories. This switch is only used when the *location* parameter is used. (New in Version 4.0.)

Shown in Fig. 2-18 is a representation of the screen during a DT session using the B(oth) option but not the /LOG option. The difference in the representation using the /LOG option is that the countdown during cluster reading and the display of the filenames during file reads are not shown. This permits printing or filing of the results neatly.

If DT finds errors in the system area of a disk, you can expect serious problems almost immediately. The best course of action is to copy carefully all of the data to another disk and discard the old disk. Reformatting the disk may correct the problem. Using WipeDisk before attempting to reformat may also eliminate the possible cause of the problem. If the problem persists after using WipeDisk and reformatting, File 13 is the only safe solution.

Sectors within a disk marked as bad are reported as "NO DANGER" by DT. DOS will mark and not use bad sectors during format.

```
A>dt

DT-Disk Test, Advanced Edition, (C) Copr 1987, Peter Norton

Select DISK test, FILE test, or BOTH
Press D, F. or B ... B

During the scan of the disk, you may press
BREAK (Control-C) to interrupt Disk Test

Test reading the entire disk A:, system area and data area
  The system area consists of boot, FAT, and directory
    No errors reading the system area

  The data area consists of clusters numbered 2 - 355
    No errors reading data area

Test reading all files
  Directory A:
    No errors reading files

A>
```

Fig. 2-18. The screen during a DT session that used the Both option but not the /LOG option.

While this can reduce the capacity of the disk, it does not mean that the disk is unsafe to use.

A problem is reported with "DANGER NOW" when DT finds an unmarked, unreadable portion of the disk within a file. This means that there may have been data written to that portion of the disk and that it may not be recoverable. Using the NU program will recover as much of the data as possible.

The warning "DANGER TO COME" is reported when DT finds a bad, unmarked sector in an area of the disk where files are not currently being stored. DT will request permission to mark the sector(s) so that DOS will not attempt to write data into these areas. This is the extent of the repair that DT can perform.

The types of checking performed by DOS's CHKDSK and DT are different. CHKDSK checks the logical order of space allocation on a disk. DT checks the ability of the disk to permit error-free reads and writes in the various areas of the disk. Using the command CHKDSK *.* /F directs the program to attempt to correct any errors found in the directory or file structures. This is an interactive process.

Before panicking, clean the heads of your floppy drive when DT reports errors. This should also be a routine part of your computer maintenance program. On a hard disk, frequent discovery of unmarked bad sectors is an indication that the hard disk is in need of repair or replacement.

When there are differences in the error reports provided by the disk-read and file-read portions of DT, it is best to copy all transferrable data onto another disk as soon as possible. Using CHKDSK may increase the amount of data that can be recovered. The disk may be reusable after it has been wiped and reformatted. Be sure to check it before writing data to it again.

When DOS reports a read error while trying to copy a file from a suspected bad disk, tell DOS to "Ignore" the error and continue. This will allow the maximum data transfer. Then use the NU program to try to rebuild the data that was lost. DT cannot correct the errors that may be caused by trying to read and transfer the data that is in a sector which DT deems "bad."

The two computer safety practices that seem to be the hardest to internalize are proper diskette care and routine, frequent backups. By *internalizing*, I mean that the habit of doing both of these things becomes so strong that they are done without consciously thinking about performing the activities.

Floppies need to be in their sleeves when they are not in the machine. They also need to be in some type of protective case when they are not in the machine. A desk full of sleeved and unsleeved floppys is an almost irresistible invitation to disaster.

Murphy's Laws are nothing if not valid. Making a backup of your hard disk is the only way to be sure that the most valuable ones won't be lost during the next thunderstorm or by some other accident of family and friends.

I know that there are files on the disk, but DOS will not read them. Is there anything I can do?

There are a number of possibilities. If you have a disk that refuses to display its directory to the DOS DIR command, there are any number of possible problems. If it is really worth the effort, run DT first to determine the extent of the problem. I just "happened" to have a disk with a problem available (Fig. 2-19).

As you can see from the results, this disk appears to have a problem with its directory. Like you, I "know" there are files on this disk. In order to verify that knowledge, I ran the NU program and took a look at the things it was able to find (Fig. 2-20).

Our claims are proved! There are files on our disks. A rather odd and perhaps interesting collection of stuff is listed. It would seem that a closer look at some of this is justified (Fig. 2-21).

While the root directory listings themselves are not all that revealing, we now know more about what was on this disk. It appears that it

---

```
C:\NU: dt a:
DT-Disk Test, Advanced Edition, (C) Copr 1987, Peter Norton

Select DISK test, FILE test, or BOTH
Press D, F, or B ... B

During the scan of the disk, you may press
BREAK (Control-C) to interrupt Disk Test

Test reading the entire disk A:, system area and data area
   The system area consists of boot, FAT, and directory
      directory area ERROR IN READING

   The data area consists of clusters numbered 2 - 355
      No errors reading data area

Test reading files
   Directory A:\ Error reading directory
      No files found

C:\NU:
```

Fig. 2-19. A screen dump in interactive mode showing a "problem" disk.

```
┌────────────────────────────────────────────────────────────────────────┐
│ Menu 1.1.3              Select file or sub-directory                     │
│                                                                          │
│                     Boot area            loader.sys                      │
│                     FAT area             msdos.sys                       │
│                 *   Root dir   *         read.me                         │
│                     00000000             sol.arc                         │
│                     11111111             sol.exe                         │
│                     88888888             term.sav                        │
│                     A                    test.2                          │
│                     CCCCCCCC             test.s                          │
│                     autoexec.bat         treeinfo.ncd                    │
│                     command.com                                          │
│                     init.sl1                                             │
│                     init.sl2                                             │
│                     init.sl3                                             │
│                     io.sys                                               │
│                                                                          │
│                      23 entries to choose from                           │
│                      Speed search:                                       │
├─────────────┬───────┬──────────────────────────────┬────────────────────┤
│ Item type   │ Drive │ Directory name               │ File name          │
│ Directory   │ A:    │ \                            │ Root dir           │
└─────────────┴───────┴──────────────────────────────┴────────────────────┘
```

Fig. 2-20. The Select File of Sub-directory menu of NU for the disk in Fig. 2-19.

┌ Root dir ═══ Directory format ┐

║ Sector 5 in root directory   Offset 0, hex 00   ║
║   Attributes   ║
║ Filename Ext   Size   Date   Time   Cluster Arc R/O Sys Hid Dir Vol ║

Filename	Ext	Size	Date	Time		Cluster	Arc	R/O	Sys	Hid	Dir	Vol
LOADER	SYS	1024	12/10/84	11:00	am	2	Arc	R/O	Sys	Hid		
IO	SYS	12037	7/15/86	6:30	pm	299	Arc	R/O	Sys	Hid		
MSDOS	SYS	17012	12/10/84	11:00	am	311	Arc	R/O	Sys	Hid		
COMMAND	COM	15957	12/10/84	11:00	am	328	Arc					
AUTOEXEC	BAT	6	4/21/87	9:32	am	344	Arc					
SOL	EXE	90240	8/05/86	12:13	am	67	Arc					
INIT	SL1	27607	4/03/86	3:57	pm	156	Arc					
INIT	SL2	27607	4/03/86	3:57	pm	183	Arc					
INIT	SL3	27607	4/03/86	3:57	pm	210	Arc					
11111111			4/02/87	3:14	pm	3					Dir	
TREEINFO	NCD	4211	4/03/87	12:57	pm	8	Arc					
88888888			4/02/87	3:18	pm	11					Dir	
00000000			4/02/87	3:18	pm	13					Dir	
CCCCCCCC			4/02/87	3:19	pm	16					Dir	
A			4/02/87	3:21	pm	20					Dir	
READ	ME	3569	7/23/86	8:25	pm	237	Arc					

```
                      Press Enter to continue
  1Help   2Hex   3Text  4Dir   5FAT   6Partn  7        8        9Undo   10QuitNU
```

Fig. 2-21. The root directory area of the disk in Fig. 2-19. (It doesn't look promising.)

started out as a bootable disk that immediately ran a program. I've made a number of these for my sons of public domain software, and this appears to have been one of them.

File Attribute

SHORT Directory Name	FA.COM
LONG Directory Name	FILEATTR.COM
Version 4.0 Directory Name	FA.EXE

Until you have this program, or one of the later versions of MS-DOS, the attributes of the files on all of the disks you own are fixed. Under many normal conditions this lack of control is not a problem, but as shown below, these attributes or characteristics do serve various purposes, and being able to change them can be of benefit to most users. The FA program is an expansion of the functions found in the MS-DOS program ATTRIB.COM.

Format   FA [d] [path/filename] [attributes & switches] [/S] [/P]
[/U] [/T]···[> | > >] [path/filename/device] (Version 3.1)

FA [d:] [path/filename] [attribute switches] [switches]
[> | > >] [path/filename/device]   (Version 4.0)

Listed below are the legal command-line options:

path/filename   The drive, path, and filename specifications for the file to be changed. Using *.* will change all of the specified files in the path.

> | > >   The DOS operators to redirect or redirect-and-append the output. There is no display when either operator is used.

path/filename|device   The target disk file or the system printer.

The file attribute switches that can be modified by FA are:

/R   Read-Only file, which normally cannot be changed or deleted.

/A   Archive file. Such files will be copied by an automatic backup program such as the DOS BACKUP program. This program also toggles this attribute off after the copy is made. DOS will turn it on again when a change is made to the file.

/SYS	Attribute of a system file, a hidden file that does not appear on the directory, and which cannot be deleted by ordinary means. DOS uses two such files on disks that are self-booting. (Ability to alter this attribute is new in Version 3.1.)
/HID	Attribute of a hidden file. These files are technically different from System files, but share the characteristic that they will not be visible on the directory and cannot be deleted by ordinary means.

These are the switches that control the functioning of the program:

+	Turns an attribute on.
−	Turns an attribute off.
/S	Instructs FA to include subdirectories in the specified path.
/P	Instructs FA to pause when the screen is full. Pressing any key will also pause the display. Pressing any key will resume the scrolling display.
/U	Instructs FA to list unusual files. "Unusual" files are those files that currently have an active attribute.
/T	Instructs FA to show only the total results. This means that the usual listing of the files and their attributes does not display.
/CLEAR	Means to remove or clear all file attributes.

If one of the attributes listed above is included without the + or − switch, it becomes part of the file description. This means that the command:

FA*.SYS/HID/R+

will add the read-only attribute to all system (.SYS) files that are also hidden files.

Part A of Fig. 2-22 shows the FA-generated directory of a sample disk. The "look" of the screen changes with Version 4.0/Advanced Edition, but the information is the same (Fig. 2-22B).

A

```
A>FA B:*.*

FA-File Attributes, Version 3.10, (C) Copr 1984-86, Peter Norton
B:\
  Hidden System Read-only Archive   LOADER.SYS
  Hidden System Read-only Archive   IO.SYS
  Hidden System Read-only Archive   MSDOS.SYS
                         Archive   COMMAND.COM
                         Archive   CAUZCOMM.COM
                         Archive   CAUZCOMM.DEF
                         Archive   EMULATE.COM
                         Archive   CLOCK.COM
                         Archive   AUTOEXEC.BAT


  9 files shown
  no files changed
```

B

```
A>


FA-File Attributes, Advanced Edition, (C) 1987, Peter Norton

  B:\
     loader.sys    Archive Read-only Hidden System
     io.sys        Archive Read-only Hidden System
     msdos.sys     Archive Read-only Hidden System
     command.com   Archive Read-only
     cauzcomm.com  Archive
     cauzcomm.def  Archive
     emulate.com   Archive
     clock.com     Archive
     autoexec.bat  Archive

  9 files shown
  no files changed

  A>
```

Fig. 2-22. Directory of a sample disk as displayed by the File Attributes utility in A) Version 3.1 and B) Version 4.0.

To protect the .COM files from change or deletion the Read-only attribute is added (Fig. 2-23A). This same command yields the display shown in Fig. 2-23B when using Version 4.0 or the Advanced Edition. The full directory display now looks like Fig. 2-24. The format change in the display for the new versions would be similar for this example also.

It would be possible to add the Hidden attribute to the COMMAND.COM, EMULATE.COM, and CLOCK.COM files so that they are not normally displayed when the DIR command is invoked.

45

```
A>FA B:*.COM /R+

FA-File Attributes, Version 3.10, (C) Copr 1984-86, Peter Norton

  B:\
                Read-only Archive  COMMAND.COM
                Read-only Archive  CAUZCOMM.COM
                Read-only Archive  EMULATE.COM
                Read-only Archive  CLOCK.COM
      4 files shown
      4 files changed
```

Ⓑ

```
FA-File Attributes, Advanced Edition, (C) Copr 1987, Peter Norton

  B:\
      command.com   Archive Read-only
      cauzcomm.com  Archive Read-only
      emulate.com   Archive Read-only
      clock.com     Archive Read-only

      4 files shown
      4 files changed

A>
```

Fig. 2-23. All the .COM files have been made read-only. Shown here are the Version 3.1 and Advanced Edition variations on the same information.

```
FA-File Attributes, Version 3.10, (C) Copr 1984-86, Peter Norton

  B:\
  Hidden System Read-only Archive  LOADER.SYS
  Hidden System Read-only Archive  IO.SYS
  Hidden System Read-only Archive  MSDOS.SYS
                Read-only Archive  COMMAND.COM
                Read-only Archive  CAUZCOMM.COM
                          Archive  CAUZCOMM.DEF
                Read-only Archive  EMULATE.COM
                Read-only Archive  CLOCK.COM
                          Archive  AUTOEXEC.BAT
```

Fig. 2-24. A post-modification full directory display.

They are called by the AUTOEXEC.BAT file. This would shorten the displayed directory.

FA without any parameters defaults to *.* and lists all of the files (and their attributes) in the currently selected directory. Note that the NU program can display more information about the attributes of any file.

The Hidden and System attributes should not normally be removed. Expert users may be able to change these attributes without causing other problems. One exception might be during a housecleaning of a hard disk. By removing these attributes, all of the files will be listed to the printer or display. Then hidden data or copy-protected or extraneous files can be deleted by normal means.

Just before backing up a series of files, it is possible to sort the backups by using the /A − and /A + switches along with various location combinations. For example:

    FA *.* /A − /S

will toggle the Archive attribute off for all files in that path. Then this command:

    FA *.DOC /A + /S

will toggle the Archive attribute on for the .DOC files in that path. After backing up those files, issue a command like:

    FA *.DAT /A + /S

to toggle the Archive attribute for the .DAT files. The Archive attribute was toggled off by the BACKUP program as it copied the .DOC files. This means that only the .DAT files will be copied on this pass. This sorted copying might provide a logical method for backing up a hard disk onto floppies.

The /CLEAR switch is equal to /A − /HID − /R − /SYS − . This means that it removes all of the active attributes from the files specified or all of the files in the specified path.

Note, too, that hiding files can be dangerous. Since they will no longer appear on the directory display they could be forgotten.

Are there any limitations on which attributes can be set for which files?

Yes, the System (/SYS) attribute should only be used with files that have an extension of .SYS. The Read-Only (/R) attribute should not be set (/R+) on any file that is subject to frequent changes.

An exception to this recommendation would be an AUTOEXEC.BAT file you didn't want changed or deleted by another user. Read-only files cannot be deleted or destroyed using WipeFile without confirmation. I've used this technique when setting up systems for new users. It prevents them from deleting everything—usually. If they learn enough to be able to change the read-only attribute, they should know better than to delete the file(s).

File Find

SHORT Directory Name   FF.COM
LONG Directory Name   FILEFIND.COM
Version 4.0 Directory Name   FF.EXE

The File Find (FF) utility locates a filename by searching through all of the directories on one or all disk drives. A partial filename or no filename may be specified. FF uses a default specification of *.* and will list all of the filenames present in the directories searched.

Format: FF [d] [filename] [d: ...] [/P] [/W] [/A] [>|>>]
[path/filename|device]   (Version 3.1)

FF[d]   [filename]   [switches]   [>|>>]   **[path/
filename|device]**   (Version 4.0)

The command parameters and switches are:

d: Indicates the drive to be searched for *filename*. Omitting the drive letter here will cause FF to search the default disk drive.

filename   The filename to be located. The wild card characters ? and * may be used with partial names, or to replace extensions. Omitting the filename will cause FF to use the default of *.* and list all filenames.

/P   Tells FF to pause when the display screen is full. Pressing any key will also pause the display; pressing a second key will resume the scrolling display.

/W   Tells FF to list the files in wide format and only show the filename. This format is five filenames wide and can display over 100 filenames at a time.

/A	Tells FF to search all of the disk drives installed in the system. (New in Version 3.1.)
> | > >	Redirect and append the program output.
path/filename/device	Specifies the redirection target, either a disk file or the system printer.

FF searches for all filenames matching the filename specified. It will search every directory and subdirectory, as well as all drives, if specified. All matches are shown along with the directory in which they are located. Hidden and system files are also displayed in FF listings. For those who store everything, FF also lists the size and time/date stamp of each filename that is matched. This means that all versions of a filename will be displayed.

Control over the extent of FF's search is exercised by specifying a drive, using the /A switch, or defaulting to the current drive. Pressing the Ctrl-Break key combination or the Esc key will abort a FF search or listing at any time without danger.

Using the DOS output redirection command allows the FF output to be sent to a disk file or the system printer. The usual method of invoking this feature is:

FF [*d:*] [*filename*] [*switches*] >[*d:*] [*new-filename\device*]

or

FF [*d:*] [*filename*] [*switches*] > >[*d:*] [*existing-filename*]

The second example will append this new FF report to the end of the report(s) or file(s) that are now in the existing filename.

Why would I ever want to find a hidden or system file?

One reason might be to check a floppy to see if the files MSDOS.COM (or IBMDOS.COM) and IOSYS.COM or (IBMBIO.COM) are on the disk. Using FF is as fast as using FA and it reports more information. Another reason might be to find other types of files that have been hidden. I hide some files using the /HID + command of FA. These files are called only by batch (.BAT) files. For me, the shorter visible directory is easier to manage.

If FA will do the same thing, why have/use FF?

FA lists all of the files in the directory or all of the files that have an active switch, while FF lists only the filename and directory. This makes the display easier to read.

How can I find out where all of the .COM files are on my hard disk?

Just ask FF to list them all for you. From the root directory (assuming that you have placed the Norton Utilities in a subdirectory called NU the command would be:

```
C:\NU\FF *.COM /W >FFCOM.LOG
```

This command runs the File Find Utility program and writes all of the .COM filenames found into a disk file called FFCOM.LOG. Since there are no other specifications on the disk file name, it will be written into the root directory. The /W switch will format the file just like the /W display. This means five across and no size or date stamp information.

By the way, why doesn't your "C" prompt look like "C>"?

I changed the prompt form C> to C:\ (directory name) so that I would always know where I was. This means that:

- C:\ is the root directory
- C:\EW: is the EasyWriter directory
- C:\NU: is the Norton Utilities directory
- C:\EW\BOOK: is the subdirectory of EW where this text is stored.

Neat! How can I do the same thing?

Add this line to the AUTOEXEC.BAT file that runs when your system boots, (which would be in the root directory). This is the same file with the SA command line to change the default colors of the background and text on your color monitor.

```
prompt       $p: $
```

The space between the "p" and the "$" is optional. I like it because it moves the cursor a space away from the text of the prompt.

Shown in Fig. 2-25 are the first few lines of two FF disk file displays. The first uses the default *.* and the second uses *.COM. Both also use the /W switch. Figure 2-26 shows a truncated dump which is the end of a 10-page listing of all of the files that were on my Drive C at the time.

```
C:\:C:\NU\FF /W

FF- File Find, Advanced Edition, (C) 1987, Peter Norton

C:\
    ibmbio.com      ibmdos.com      DOS             NU              R5K
    ARC             EW              PKX             PAS             BAS
    FASTBACK        GAME            DIAG            BACKIT          QDOS
    MACE            DBASE           MISC            AMU             auto.bat
    autotemp.bat    ansi.sys        fileinfo.fi     treeinfo.ncd    qd2.log
    config.sys      savscr.com      command.com     autoexec.bak    master.mdf
    utility.mdf     lang.mdf        game.mdf        dir.log         autoexec.bat

C:\QDOS

C:\:C\NU\FF *.COM /W

FF- File Find, Advanced Edition (C) 1987, Peter Norton

C:\
    ibmbio.com      ibmdos.com      savscr.com      command.com

C:\DOS
    assign.com      backup.com      chkdsk.com      comp.com        debug.com
    fdisk.com       format.com      keyb.com        edlin.com       mode.com
    command.com     restore.com     label.com       select.com      sys.com
    recover.com     graphics.com    diskcomp.com    diskcopy.com    print.com
    tree.com        more.com        graftabl.com

C:\ARC
    arce.com        autocust.com    automenu.com    sw.com

C:\EW

58 files found
```

Can I also search for just the hidden files?

Fig. 2-25. Typical File Find screen displays, truncated to only a few lines.

Yes, as long as you know the filenames. The same is true of system and "signature" files.

Is there a possibility that I will damage anything with all of my searching?

No, FF will not damage anything. Only the usually occurring accidents and acts of God (or the local power company) can be expected to cause damage.

```
FF- File Find, Advanced Edition (C) 1987, Peter Norton

        zipcode.ndx        2,048 bytes    9:00 am   Thu Dec 26 85

C:\MISC
        .                  <DIR>          8:12 pm   Mon Jul  6 87
        ..                 <DIR>          8:12 pm   Mon Jul  6 87
        wcx.arc            1,280 bytes   12:30 am   Sat Jun 13 87
        wcx.com              553 bytes    1:17 am   Tue Jun 10 86
        wcx.doc            1,029 bytes    6:40 am   Mon Jun  9 86
        msspad.com         1,641 bytes   12:05 am   Tue Jan  1 80
        msspad.doc         1,340 bytes   12:17 am   Tue Jan  1 80
        masspad.arc        1,920 bytes   12:28 am   Sat Jun 13 87

C:\AMU
        .                  <DIR>         11:19 pm   Fri Jul 10 87
        ..                 <DIR>         11:19 pm   Fri Jul 10 87
        automenu.com      17,214 bytes   12:10 am   Sat Jul 11 87
        autocust.com       9,311 bytes    4:01 am   Fri May 15 87
        automake.exe      78,956 bytes    4:01 am   Fri May 15 87
        dos.mdf            4,072 bytes    4:01 am   Fri May 15 87
        automenu.mdf       1,510 bytes   12:16 am   Sat Jul 11 87
        autotemp.bat         256 bytes   12:17 am   Sat Jul 11 87
        auto.bat             171 bytes   12:12 am   Sat Jul 11 87

559 files found
```

Fig. 2-26. The default listing format and content of FF, truncated to the last few lines.

File Information

The File Information utility permits the addition of descriptive comments to the DOS filename, which can be displayed by using the FI command rather than the DOS DIR command. Computers that are not fully IBM-compatible must use EMULATE.COM or a similar utility to use this program.

Note: Don't confuse the name of the program ("eff-eye") with the name of a key ("eff-one").

Format: FI [*path/filename*] [*comments*] [*switches*]

The following command-line options are available:

path/filename   The specific file to which the comment is to to be attached. The default (*.*) will display all of the files in the root directory of the currently selected drive. This is the interactive mode and FI will display each filename in order. If no comment is to be added or edited, pressing Return will display the next filename.

comment   The text of the comment to be attached to the filename selected.

The switches available are:

/C   Tells FI to list only those files that already have comments attached.

/D   Tells FI that the comment attached to *path/filename* is to be deleted.

/E   Tells FI that a comment is to be edited or entered. The *path/filename* parameter is required in this case. Maximum comment length is 65 characters.

/L	Tells FI to display a long format. This means that the entire comment will be shown.
/N	Used with computers that are not fully IBM-compatible. (This is a case where my TI PC is fully compatible.)
/P	Tells FI to pause when the screen is full.
/PACK	A utility that compresses the data in the comment file.
/S	Tells FI to include the subdirectories of the selected drive and directory.

Figure 2-27 is a partial screen dump using the B:FI /L command. Without the /L option, the display looks like Fig. 2-28. The size and date stamp information is not shown when the full comment is displayed. Using the FI command alone allows only the first 36 characters to

Fig. 2-27. A screen dump using the FI command with the /L switch active.

```
A>FI B: /L

FI-File Information, Advanced Edition, (C) 1987, Peter Norton

DIAG
BACKIT
QDOS
MACE
DBASE
MISC
AMU
auto     bat
autotemp bat
ansi     sys
fileinfo fi    the file holding all of these comments
treeinfo ncd
qd2      log
config   sys
savscr   com   Saves a screen to a disk file
command  com
master   mdf
utility  mdf
lang     mdf
game     mdf
autoexec bat
```

FI-File Information, Advanced Edition, (C) 1987, Peter Norton

DIAG		<DIR>	1-01-80	12:01a	
BACKIT		<DIR>	1-01-80	12:03a	
QDOS		<DIR>	7-05-87	7:42p	
MACE		<DIR>	1-01-80	12:08a	
DBASE		<DIR>	7-06-87	7:49p	
MISC		<DIR>	7-06-87	8:12p	
AMU		<DIR>	7-10-87	11:19p	
auto	bat	176	7-10-87	11:17p	
autotemp	bat	128	7-10-87	11:18p	
ansi	sys	1,678	3-17-87	12:00p	
fileinfo	fi	753	6-27-87	8:43p	the file holding all of these commen
treeinfo	ncd	203	7-10-87	11:19p	
qd2	log	3,206	7-05-87	7:46p	
config	sys	28	7-06-87	3:22p	
savscr	com	2,048	7-06-87	8:56p	Saves a screen to a disk file
command	com	26,624	7-06-87	8:56p	
master	mdf	508	7-10-87	11:46p	
utility	mdf	579	7-10-87	11:54p	
lang	mdf	392	7-10-87	11:57p	
game	mdf	564	7-11-87	12:07a	
autoexec	bat	59	7-11-87	4:50p	

Fig. 2-28. An FI-generated screen dump with no switches active.

A>FI B:treeinfo.ncd /E

FI-File Info, Advanced Edition, (C) Copr 1987, Peter Norton

```
 Directory:  B:\
 File name:  treeinfo.ncd
   Comment:
                        Press  Esc  to  quit
```

Fig. 2-29. A File Information display in interactive or editing mode.

be displayed. Not even this partial display of characters appears when
the DOS DIR command is used.

Figure 2-29 is a screen display obtained by executing this command:

FI B:treeinfo.ncd /E

Before entering the text, the comment line was blank. Pressing Return writes the comment into the FILEINFO.FI, file which becomes
part of the indicated directory. It is possible to replace all use of the
DOS DIR command with the FI command. There are advantages to

this choice. FI/L will display all of the comments attached to the filenames, pressing any key (except Esc or F10) will pause the display, pressing Return will display filenames one line at a time, and pressing the space bar will display filenames one page at a time. Pressing any other key will return the display to the normal auto-scroll mode.

Being able to attach comments to DOS filenames can be very useful when faced with filenames as informative as some of the following:

EMW0700Q0.LOD
EMW0710RT.LOD
DK93001V3.COM
XBA6802M2.EXE

With descriptive commenting, these filenames no longer are just so many characters once the reasoning behind the cryptic notation has grown cold. It can also prove very useful when files are compressed. The comment can clearly indicate the contents of the file when the filename doesn't.

Within the editing box (displayed in response to using the /E switch), the following WordStar-compatible commands are available:

[Ctrl-RightArrow]	Cursor right one word
[Ctrl-F]	Cursor right one word
[Ctrl-LeftArrow]	Cursor left one word
[Ctrl-A]	Cursor left one word
[Home]	Cursor to beginning of line
[RightArrow]	Cursor right one character
[Ctrl-D]	Cursor right one character
[LeftArrow]	Cursor left one character
[Ctrl-S]	Cursor left one character
[Backspace]	Delete one character left
[Del]	Delete character under cursor
[Ctrl-T]	Delete word right
[Ctrl-W]	Delete word left
[Ctrl-Y]	Delete entire line
[Esc]	Abort
[F10]	Abort
[F1]	Display next filename

Note: There are two possibilities for most of the commands. This allows you to use the more comfortable or familiar combination. The command FI [path/filename] /D also will delete the existing comment for filename.

When adding or editing comments for more than one file (the FI /E command), pressing the Return key will complete the activity on the indicated filename and clear the FI program. By pressing the F1 key, it's possible to single-step through the entire directory adding, editing or deleting comments before clearing FI.

The FILEINFO.FI file will automatically compact itself at some point in time. What it is actually doing is restoring the data into contiguous sectors. Fragmentation of files often occurs on disks where there are many "writes" and/or "deletes." The /PACK switch does for FILEINFO.FI what the DS utility program does for the entire disk.

Can you give me some examples of when you might use FI to tag comments to filenames?

I use electronic mail extensively. Most of my messages are created off-line and then transferred to DELPHI via a protocol. To keep things simple, I usually just use the person's username as the filename; a number is included if there is more than one message to that individual. The date is used as the extension. This serves the dual roles of identification and providing a common factor for batch transfers (*.nnn). The numbers are adequate to describe the day and the month. Putting FI comments on each of these files saves time later when I try to determine if the message should be saved for days or months.

Archive-type files that have been compressed using ARC or another compression utility can contain numerous source files. FI lets me indicate the contents more efficiently than using the "L" or "V" commands. Even then, these two commands will only give the filenames. I find the descriptive comments much more useful.

Can I still use DIR and DIR/W after using FI?

Yes. FI creates FILEINFO.FI, where the comments records are stored. When you use FI you will not see that file. Using DIR or DIR/W will display it.

What are the practical limits of FI?

Each comment is limited to 65 characters and each file is limited to one comment. Beyond that, only disk space can limit FI.

Does FILEINFO.FI retain the comments that I had on a file that was deleted?

Yes and no. Immediately after the filename was deleted, the comment is still on file. If the /PACK switch is used, however, the comment records of deleted files will be eliminated. FI will also perform a pack when it reaches a certain point. Packing eliminates unnecessary comment records and thereby improves response time.

If I delete a filename by mistake and recover it using QU, will FI still be able to display the comment I had for it?

Yes, as long as a pack has not been done by you or FI while the file was deleted.

Format Recovery

This utility will undo the apparent damage done by the accidental reformatting of most hard disks, allowing the recovery of the information that was on the disk. Exceptions are Compaq DOS 3.1 and AT&T DOS 2.11, which overwrite the disk during formatting. Version 3.2 DOS for the Compaq and AT&T systems should correct this problem. The recovery file FRECOVER.DAT must also have been prepared before attempting to do this recovery operation.

Format: FR [*d:*] [*switches*]

where *d:* is the hard disk to be recovered. The following *switches* are available:

/SAVE   Prepares the file FRECOVER.DAT to be used in the recovery attempt.

(blank)   When FR is called without any switch being specified, it will look first for the FRECOVER.DAT file and then attempt to recover the format and information on the disk drive specified. No drive specification will default to the currently selected drive.

Losing all of the information stored on one of today's multimegabyte hard disks can be very traumatic. Rationalizations can be made for defective equipment, power failures, and many other incidents that can cause hard disk failures. Entering a FORMAT command or having a "Trojan Horse" program reformat the hard disk for you cannot be justified.

Including the FR [*d:*] /SAVE command in an AUTOEXEC.BAT file will ensure that hard disk recovery information is available and current. The ability of FR to recover information from a hard disk that has had nothing done to it since the FORMAT command was issued is totally dependent on the information in the FRECOVER.DAT file.

FR is not designed to replace the systematic backing up of hard disk files. It is much like the UnErase utility available for file recovery—a last chance.

FR works only on hard disks, and only within the limits stated. It would also be very prudent to keep the FRECOVER.DAT file on a floppy, not on the hard disk subject to a possible FORMAT command error. In spite of all of the advances being made in hardware and software, there is nothing that will replace the security and importance of regular housekeeping. The hardware needs maintenance as does the software.

Where should I keep my latest copy of FRECOVER.DAT?

Keep it on a separate, bootable floppy disk! If your hard disk has been reformatted, accidentally or otherwise, FR will not be able to locate any filenames on that disk (Fig. 2-30).

Notice that there is a file called REC.EXE on this floppy. This is actually FR.EXE renamed. I've made use of the FR filename in the .BAT batch file. The single command line rec c:/s is sufficient to have the program build a new FRECOVER.DAT file on the hard disk. Then using the copy command it can be transferred to the floppy.

```
C:\: dir a:

Volume in drive A is frecover
Directory of  A:\

IBMBIO    COM    22100   3-18-87   12:00p
IBMDOS    COM    30159   3-17-87   12:00p
COMMAND   COM    25307   3-17-87   12:00p
REC       EXE    12500   5-15-87    4:00p
FRECOVER  DAT    61440   7-15-87    1:31p
FR        BAT       11   1-01-80   12:17a
        6 File(s)    207872 bytes free

C:\: type a:fr.bat
rec c:/s
```

Fig. 2-30. Directory of a sample diskette for using the FR utility. (Note that IBMBIO.COM and IBMDOS.COM normally are hidden files.)

Does that mean that I have to remember to get that disk out to update the .DAT file?

It does, unless you put a bit of code into an ASK file. If the menu selection says "(B)ackup," the action code could be:

A:FR c:/SAVE (/S will also work)

If the disk isn't there, an error message will display. This same line could be the action code for the (Q)uit selection used just before shutting down the system.

Can I recover the data on a reformatted disk without a FRECOVER.DAT file?

An expert working under ideal conditions might be able to salvage a significant portion. NU in the maintenance (/M) mode may be able to recover data sector by sector. Text files are relatively easy to read. It's the compiled code files that cause the greatest problems.

Is there any way to prevent "Trojan Horse" programs from being able to reformat my hard disk?

Yes, there are a couple of things that you can do. One would be to rename the FORMAT.COM program, although any Trojan Horse worth its salt would access the disk via machine code calls rather than from the command line. Another, and better, way is to screen all of the programs you receive from a bulletin board or a questionable source with a program that reads the ASCII strings in the new file.

The sick minds that develop "Trojan Horses" also require recognition. They get it by leaving some type of a message, usually as an ASCII string, to let you know that they have just destroyed your many hours of hard work. There are a number of these little utilities in the public domain; one of the best-known is called CHK4BOMB. Most of the subscription services, like DELPHI and BIX, as well as many of the more active local BBS systems will have some type of "checker" program available.

File Size

SHORT Directory Name	**FS.COM**
LONG Directory Name	**FILESIZE.COM**
Version 4.0 Directory Name	**FS.EXE**

DS displays the amount of disk space occupied by the files in a directory. DS also displays amount of *slack* (dead space) currently included in the file space. DS also can look at a target disk and report on the amount of space available and whether there is enough for a copy of the named file. Redirection is available and useful when checking a hard disk with the default *.* parameter and the /S switch active.

Format: FS [*path/filename*] [*d:*] [/P] [/T] [/S] [>|>>]
[*path/filename|device*]   (Version 3)

FS [*path/filename*] [*d:*] [*switches*] [>|>>]
[*path/filename|device*]   (Version 4.)

The command-line parameters and switches are:

path/filename   The file(s) to be sized and their location. If no filename is specified, the *.* default applies. If no path is specified, the default is the root directory.

d: The target drive letter. When not specified, the currently selected drive is searched. This switch is used to check for open disk space before copying a file to the disk in this drive.

/P   Tells FS to pause when the display screen is full. If you forget to include this option, pressing any key will pause the display. Pressing a second key will resume the scrolling display.

/S   Tells FS to include all subdirectories in its search for filename. (New in Version 3.1.)

/T   Tells FS to display/report totals only. This means that individual file sizes will not be included. Using this switch together with redirection reduces the size of the report file significantly.

>|>>   The DOS operators to redirect or redirect-and-append the program output. There is no display when either of these operators is used.

path/filename/device   The redirection target, either a disk file or the system printer.

The default search criterion for FS is *.* on the currently selected drive. This means that it will report on all of the files in the currently selected directory of the currently selected drive.

A printout of an FS report (Version 3.*x*) would look something like part A of Fig. 2-31. In Version 4.0 this same type of report would

---

A

```
FS-File Size, Version 3.10, (C) Copr 1984-86, Peter Norton

   A:\
         2,444 BEEP.COM
        15,957 COMMAND.COM
         7,724 DS.COM
         7,522 DT.COM
    - etc. -

       262,705 total bytes in 27 files in A:\
       276,480 bytes disk space occupied, 5% slack
```

B

```
FS-File Size, Advanced Edition, (C) Copr 1987, Peter Norton


   A:\
     loader.sys        1,024 bytes
     ask.exe           1,270 bytes
     beep.exe          4,688 bytes
     ds.exe           25,474 bytes
    - etc. -

       269,548 total bytes in 25 files
       281,600 bytes disk space occupied, 4% slack

Drive usage
       362,496 bytes available on drive A:
        80,896 bytes unused on drive A:   22% unused
```

Fig. 2-31. Typical File Size reports in Versions 3.1 and 4.0.

look similar to part B. I find the added three lines on drive usage are perhaps the most valuable addition.

The way disk space is managed means there will be some slack space on every disk. The total amount of slack must be minimal for efficient disk usage. The utility program SD (speed disk) is designed to make maximum use of the space available on any DOS disk, floppy or hard. There are also compression programs that will reduce the size of files that are being placed on disk for storage purposes. Careful usage of both will ensure that your disks hold every last bit of information that can be packed on them.

Slack space is a function of the file size versus the space allocation scheme being used by DOS. These schemes vary with the version of DOS and the type of disk. Allocations currently range from 1K clusters on a standard 360K floppy to 8K clusters on a DOS 2.x formatted hard disk. DOS 3.x, where available, can format hard disks using a 2K cluster. This can provide a dramatic slack space reduction on disks having many small files. *Remember! Always back up your hard disk before reformatting!*

I just used SD to unfragment all of the files on my hard disk. When I run FS, it still shows one directory with over 30 percent slack, is there something wrong?

I doubt it, if this is a constant thing with this directory. Briefly, what you are seeing is a report of the blank spaces at the end of each file. This usually indicates there are many small files in the directory.

Is there any way to reduce this slack space?

Reducing cluster size is the only way. However, that is set by the FORMAT command. If there is a different version of FORMAT available with a smaller cluster size, it is a worthwhile investment.

If the cluster were reduced to one sector (512 bytes) what would happen?

It would take longer to read the hard disk, and it would reduce the number of bytes that could be stored. The reduction would be due to addressing problems, not the inability of the disk to hold them. Current DOS addressing techniques provide addresses for 32 megabytes of hard disk storage. Larger disks are divided into different "logical" drives. This means that a single hard disk assembly (a "physical" drive) could actually be 2, 3, or even more drives electrically.

66

Can you give me an example of how to check a disk for adequate space before trying to copy the file?

The illustrations shown in Fig. 2-32 provide the clearest way to explain how to do it and what to expect. The upper display indicates that there is enough space on that disk for the file named DBASE.OVL, while in the second example there is not enough space.

Are there files with 0 percent slack?

One such file is used in Fig. 2-32.

Is there any type of file that cannot be checked by FS?

Every type of file that DOS can read or write to can be checked by FS.

```
C:\DBASE: c:\nu\fs dbase.ovl a:
FS-File Size, Advanced Edition, (C) Copr 1987, Peter Norton

   C:\DBASE
      dbase.ovl        272,384 bytes

      272,384 bytes disk space occupied, 0% slack

      272,384 bytes disk space needed to copy to A:
      287,744 bytes available on A:, enough disk space

 Drive usage
   21,309,440 bytes available on drive C:
   13,281,280 bytes unused on drive C:, 62% unused

C:\DBASE:
```

```
C:\DBASE: c:\nu\fs dbase.ovl a:
FS-File Size, Advanced Edition, (C) Copr 1987, Peter Norton

   C:\DBASE
      dbase.ovl        272,384 bytes

      272,384 bytes disk space occupied, 0% slack

      272,384 bytes disk space needed to copy to A:
       57,344 bytes available on A:, insufficient disk space

 Drive usage
   21,309,440 bytes available on drive C:
   13,281,280 bytes unused on drive C:, 62% unused
```

Fig. 2-32. File Size screen dumps showing A) enough space to execute a copy operation to Drive A:, and B) insufficient space on the target drive.

List Directories

SHORT Directory Name	**LD.COM**
LONG Directory Name	**LISTDIR.COM**
Version 4.0 Directory Name	**LD.EXE**

This utility is designed to make it easier to display all of the directories and subdirectories present on a disk. LD is especially useful when attempting to manage large hard disk systems. With Version 4.0, a graphic capability has been added.

Format: LD *[d:]* [/p] [/W] [> | > >] [*device\filename*]
(Version 3.0)

LD [*d:*] [/A] [/P] [/W] [/T] [> | > >] [*device\filename*]
(Version 3.1)

LD [*d:*] [*pathname*] [*switches*] [> | > >] [*device\file-
name*]   (Version 4.0 and AE)

The following command-line options are available:

d: Indicates the drive from which LD is to get the directory information.

pathname   Selects a path within a disk to be listed. This new switch allows you to obtain partial listings.

Fig. 2-33 shows an LD report with no switches active. The operation of LD may be modified with the following:

/A   List the directories of all drives.

/G   Display the directory tree graphically (Fig 2-34).

/N   Used with the /G switch when redirecting the output to a printer that does not support the IBM extended character set.

/P   Pause the display after each filled display screen. Pressing any key will also pause the display if this switch has not been included on the command line.

```
C:\: c:\util\nu\ld
LD-List Directories, Advanced Edition, (C) Copr 1987, Peter Norton

   C:\ (root)
   C:\UTIL
   C:\UTIL\NU
   C:\UTIL\PCT
   C:\UTIL\ARC
   C:\UTIL\METRO
   C:\UTIL\QD2
   C:\DOS
   C:\EW
   C:\EW\BKNU
   C:\GAME

11 directories

   C:\:
```

Fig. 2-33. A typical List Directories (LD) screen with no switches active.

```
C:LD/g
LD-List Directories, Advanced Edition, (C) Copr 1987, Peter Norton

C:\───┬─UTIL────────┬─NU
      │             ├─PCT
      │             ├─ARC
      │             ├─METRO
      │             └─QD2
      ├─DOS
      ├─EW──────────────BKNU
      └─GAME

11 directories
```

Fig. 2-34. An LD "graphics" screen.

/T	Display the total number and total size of the files in each directory, in addition to the directory listing (Fig. 2-35). Filenames are not displayed.
/W	Display the directory listing in wide format. This switch is not operational in Version 4.0.
>	The DOS redirection operator used to send the output of LD to a printer or disk file. DOS will create the file if it does not exist, or overwrite if it does.

```
C:\: c:\util\nu\ld /t
LD-List Directories, Advanced Edition, (C) Copr 1987, Peter Norton

    C:\ (root)
        12 files total 109,537 bytes
    C:\UTIL
         0 files
    C:\UTIL\NU
        26 files total 468,289 bytes
    C:\UTIL\PCT
        11 files total 297,754 bytes
    C:\UTIL\ARC
        02 files total 37,894 bytes
    C:\UTIL\METRO
        35 files total 442,814 bytes
    C:\UTIL\QD2
        05 files total 222,849 bytes
    C:\DOS
        51 files total 532,287 bytes
    C:\EW
        55 files total 1,021,998 bytes
    C:\EW\BKNU
        45 files total 336,852 bytes
    C:\GAME
        19 files total 306,734 bytes

 11 directories containing 261 files totalling 3,777,008 bytes
```

> > DOS redirection operator which appends the new information to an existing file. This operator is normally used only with disk files. DOS will create the file if it does not exist.

Fig. 2-35. The file generated by LD using the /T switch and DOS redirection.

device/filename Where the redirected output is to be sent. The redirections >PRN or >LPTI will produce a hard copy of the output of LD. For file output, the redirection > >A:dir.lst will write the output of LD to the end of the file named DIR.LST in Drive A. These selections are usually mutually exclusive, meaning that you should select one or the other.

Line Print

SHORT Directory Name	**LP.COM**
LONG Directory Name	**LINEPRNT.COM**
Version 4.0 Directory Name	**LP.EXE**

LP provides a simple means of printing text files. Although similar to the DOS PRINT or TYPE commands, LP offers formatting options that are not available with either of the other commands. LP is *not* a word processor, however.

Format: LP   [*d:*]   [*path*]   *filename*   [*device*]   [*switches*]

The command-line options for the LP (formerly LPRINT) command are:

[*d:*] [*path*] *filename*   The location and name of the file(s) which are to be used as the input for LP. More than one file may be specified by using the DOS wildcard characters.

device   The printer or drive/path/filename which is to receive the output of LP. If a filename is specified, wildcard characters must not be used.

/T*n*   The number of lines to allow for the top margin. The default value in Version 4.0 is 3.

/B*n*   The number of lines to allow for the bottom margin. The default value in Version 4.0 is 5.

/L*n*   The number of columns to allow for the left margin. The default value in Version 4.0 is 5.

/R*n*   The number of columns to allow for the right margin. The default value in Version 4.0 is 5.

/H*n*   The page length in lines. The default in Version 4.0 is 66.

/W*n*   The width of the page in columns. The default value in Version 4.0 is 85.

/S*n*	The line spacing to be used. The default value in Version 4.0 is 1.
/P*n*	The starting page number. The default value in Version 4.0 is 1.
/N	The line numbering toggle. The default value in Version 3.0 and later is Off. This means that you must include this switch when you want the line numbers printed.
/80	The page width toggle. The default value in Version 4.0 is On. This means that the /W switch and value are used only when the page width is any value other than 80 or the /132 switch is being used.
/132	The compressed print toggle. Using this switch will preface the text to be printed with the IBM printer codes to enable the compressed print mode in compatible printers.
/HEADER*n*	Sets the header to be printed on each page. Values are: 0 = no headers; 1 = current time and date are printed; 2 = current time and date plus the file time and date. The default value in Version 4.0 is 1.
/EBCDIC	Tells LP that the file to be printed is in EBCDIC code. LP will convert the coding to ASCII and print the "printable" characters. The default value of this toggle is Off.
/EXT	This toggle tells LP to print the extended character set, assuming that the printer is compatible. This includes the European character set. The default setting in Version 4.0 is Off. This means that the eighth bit of each byte is stripped off by LP in the default mode.
/SET:*drive/path/filename*	Tells LP where to find a format file with the switch settings to be used for the current task. This is a file you must develop. There is no default value for this switch.

One useful task that LP can perform is the printing of READ.ME-type files that are not received in "ready-to-print" form.

Using a text file such as TEST.TXT (shown in Fig. 2-36), we can demonstrate some of the features available within LP. Entering the following command:

A>1p b:test.txt b:default

produces the output shown in Fig. 2-37. Adding the double-spacing switch (/S2) to the command line forms the command:

1p b:test.txt b:stest /n/s2

Fig. 2-36. The sample ASCII text file used for the next four illustrations.

and yields a double spaced and numbered copy (Fig. 2-38). This type of printout can be very useful when writing programs and the editor does not print out the line numbers.

```
This text is being used to display the various options available using the
NORTON UTILITIES program LP (LinePrint). The bulk of this text file is just
random key strokes to fill space. For those options where the length of this
file runs overa single page the balance of the file has been truncated. There
is nothing in the portions omitted that cannot be seen in the remainder.

This line is exactly 80 characters long - asdrqweradfgwerasdfhrtaefsdfgwegaerrx.

This line is 120 characters long - poiujhasdfnqwer;oizxxcvnesr;oixzx ;lwerbasdlkjasdfuhvlkjerbzx

This line is 132 characters long - l;knv weihoc qwer;kjuisdfmcawekjnzdscdoiretnasdfpoiuwertbasddp

This is a random paragraph. weroixf l;kjjeertv zd louiwe4trlkdfguiol sdf ;kesrt
asdlfkjn asdf;lkasdf asdlkugv aser;lkasdfvbnlasdf dhliu asd aeertkjuzd vdfl;ka
flk j ads;lk;vt asdfkjuert. nsdfiusdfv x lksdfg sdfg;lkasc sdfgl kjxfbnger tl;
sdfgkjlcv erlkjsdfgowertbsd sdfg lsdkfglkj dfbp apjtr asdf;kjdzcv. dasf;kjzvc
asdf ljasdf;jkat asdlkcvb drg  sefoiijxcvb ers;osdfsg  asr;lk ;c asdjkdfgnweaa
asd;j ;alertnzxfvuioetr sdfg;kjsd sdfg;kjlert dfg;serty sdf; asdlkjterpoiu cs
asd;lkfgoiuwert ertypoiuxfb sdtipou pewewrt wepoiucvb sdyfpo ser werpoisdfgsvs
aeropliev  wertlku  oieurtbe vytreopixc sstdpoiwer v fgdspoiuwert servpoiweryu
drgpoise c;oiertycvp[osdfg sertpoi sdywpoifgb sdpoisdfb wetpoiusdfcgv sertgps
sdf vpsrt sdfgpiu sgfhrtyyu seopidb w5nm sdfgp sertynshtp poimsdy sp rgyertsdg
ty;oxdf rtypoifgh ertpdfgnbnmrte wep dfghwr sdfgpoi dfty4erdfghb rtypdfghs rydf
si sfgh dfghl;kfty dftypwerty dfgh;pldfghdsfln pijn  poiubn rtypm s d wetrypo
This is line 25. aeropi qpertioun asertoidsffg aertpoi dsa

cmmlert  opiumsert ertldgfhh yuirety dfghjc ponsdvpioiet sefvprty xsdv oiwert
errt csdfgopity dfghbpotry sdfpoi pserty c pidstfg p pn wertyl; jert eyrtwe
adgbnopijretg brtyoi erfv evop rto nprtg wero  esrtopv lert sdolhb terodfgs
er  liretnsdfoib ertgoisdfnert ertopb ttrgeoijxd srty sert bgsdf bbytyr erbs
sddfg rttyr  loesrty erto biurt ertybos welioughg woibv h6eolisdr erslb slijr
sergcv erpiouesrtg wloxfv serloig serlokgh sei ljsder vrteop`loijer eroijn ssdfg
dd sdfgfgb tyloxc dlo iondtyu drtyl;cfg rtylxf errtykvb ertyyrt dfgertfy hjhn
dfg ,c .trynpxf njiutfyko jiyuu vh o gtf hni hkjjj yut l,,ofgh v ltrnxitrnvmtd
This is line 35. gfcertkn nmeert  dfhj ervklert xvkdrty cfksdty xvdkrt rtoidf.
This is the end of this file.
```

This text is being used to display the various options available using the NORTON UTILITIES program LP (LinePrint). The bulk of this text file is just random key strokes to fill space. For those options where the length of thi
s
file runs overa single page the balance of the file has been truncated. The
re
is nothing in the portions omitted that cannot be seen in the remainder.

This line is exactly 80 characters long - asdrqweradfgwerasdfhrtaefsdfgwega errx.

This line is 120 characters long - poiujhasdfnqwer;oizxxcvnesr;oixzx ;lwerb asdlkjasdfuhvlkjerbzx oiurtnasdfasdrsagezsvt.

This line is 132 characters long - l;knv weihoc qwer;kjuisdfmcawekjnzdscdoi retnasdfpoiuwertbasddpfoitrbnasdfpoitrkjsdeuiretblzsdfde.

This is a random paragraph. weroixf l;kjjeertv zd louiwe4trlkdfguiol sdf ;k esrt

Fig. 2-37. The default output format of Line Print.

1 This text is being used to display the various options available us

   ing the

2 NORTON UTILITIES program LP (LinePrint). The bulk of this text file

   is just

3 random key strokes to fill space. For those options where the lengt

   h of this

4 file runs overa single page the balance of the file has been trunca

   ted. There

5 is nothing in the portions omitted that cannot be seen in the remai

   nder.

Fig. 2-38. Output of LP with the /N and /S2 switches active.

Where very long lines are anticipated, the /132 switch can be useful. This will switch most printers to the "condensed print" mode (Fig. 2-39). Keeping the line numbering switched on still leaves room for about 120 to 125 characters per line.

All of the example files shown above have the default HEADER1. The next example (Fig. 2-40) was produced using the command string:

```
1p b:test.txt b:2head /header2/110/r10/t6
```

This output looks a bit more like a standard letter format. The top and side margins are about one inch each, and bottom margin is a bit more.

Versions 3.0 and 3.1 both have the LP program. The default output of LP in both of these versions mirrors Version 4.0.

More on the Setup File. The control codes in this file are sent to the printer before text printing actually begins. In effect, this

Fig. 2-39. LP output with the /132 switch active.

TEST.TXT   Saturday, August 8, 1987   Page 1

This text is being used to display the various options available using the NORTON UTILITIES program LP (LinePrint). The bulk of this text file is just random key strokes to fill space. For those options where the length of this file runs overa single page the balance of the file has been truncated. There is nothing in the portions omitted that cannot be seen in the remainder.

This line is exactly 80 characters long - asdrqweradfgwerasdfhrtaefsdfgwegaerrx.

This line is 120 characters long - poiujhasdfnqwer;oizxxcvnesr;oixzx ;lwerbasdlkjasdfuhvlkjerbzx oiurtnasdfasdrsagezsvt.

This line is 132 characters long - l;knv weihoc qwer;kjuisdfmcawekjnzdscdoiretnasdfpoiuwertbasddpfoitrbnasdfpoitrkjsdeuire tblzsdfde.

This is a random paragraph. weroixf l;kjjeertv zd louiwe4trlkdfguiol sdf ;kesrt asdlfkjn asdf;lkasdf asdlkugv aser;lkasdfvbnlasdf dhliu asd aeertkjuzd vdfl;ka flk j ads;lk;vt asdfkjuert. nsdfiusdfv x lksdfg sdfg;lkasc sdfgl kjxfbnger tl; sdfgkjlcv erlkjsdfgowertbsd sdfg lsdkfglkj dfbp apjtr asdf;kjdzcv. dasf;kjzvc asdf ljasdf;jkat asdlkcvb drg sefoiijxcvb ers;osdfsg asr;lk ;c asdjkdfgnweaa asd;j ;alertnzxfvuioetr sdfg;kjsd sdfg;kjlert dfg;serty sdf; asdlkjterpoiu cs asd;lkfgoiuwert ertypoiuxfb sdtipou pewewrt wepoiucvb sdyfpo ser werpoisdfgsvs aeropliev wertlku oieurtbe vytreopixc sstdpoiwer v fgdspoiuwert servpoiweryu drgpoise c;oiertycvp[osdfg sertpoi sdywpoifgb sdpoisdfb wetpoiusdfcgv sertgps sdf vpsrt sdfgpiu sgfhrtyyu seopidb w5nm sdfgp sertynshtp poimsdy sp rgyertsdg ty;oxdf rtypoifgh ertpdfgnbnmrte wep dfghwr sdfgpoi dfty4erdfghb rtypdfghs rydf si sfgh dfghl;kfty dftypwerty dfgh;pldfghdsfln pijn poiubn rtypm s d wetrypo This is line 25. aeropi qpertioun asertoidsffg aertpoi dsa

---

75

```
TEST.TXT              Saturday, August 8, 1987            Page 1
              File Created: Saturday, August 8, 1987 at 6:37 pm

This text is being used to display the various options available
using the
NORTON UTILITIES program LP (LinePrint). The bulk of this text fi
le is just
random key strokes to fill space. For those options where the len
gth of this
file runs overa single page the balance of the file has been trun
cated. There
is nothing in the portions omitted that cannot be seen in the rem
ainder.

This line is exactly 80 characters long - asdrqweradfgwerasdfhrta
efsdfgwegaerrx.

This line is 120 characters long - poiujhasdfnqwer;oizxxcvnesr;oi
xzx ;lwerbasdlkjasdfuhvlkjerbzx oiurtnasdfasdrsagezsvt.

This line is 132 characters long - l;knv weihoc qwer;kjuisdfmcawe
kjnzdscdoiretnasdfpoiuwertbasddpfoitrbnasdfpoitrkjsdeuiretblzsdfd
e.
```

file becomes a device driver. Control code format for this file follows the Lotus 1-2-3 convention. Note the use of the backslash "\".

Fig. 2-40. Output of Line Print with the /HEADER2 switch active.

\ *nnn*	Where *n* equals the decimal number of the code. Three numbers are required. This means that padding with leading zeros may be required.
\ *c*	Where *c* is the control character. This means that ^A = Ctrl-A = \A.
c	Where *c* is any character to be sent to the printer to be printed.

One extension (addition) to the Lotus format is included in the Norton Utilities implementation. You may separate control codes with a carriage return. This means you may press the Return key so that the codes appear on separate lines in the file. If a carriage return is to be sent to the printer, then the string "\013" must be included in the file.

A carriage return on the IBM PC is really a carriage return and a line feed. This means that both codes, the "\013" carriage return and the "\010" line feed codes must be included in the setup file to duplicate the usual reaction seen when pressing the Return key.

The following example files are equivalents:

    \AThis is a setup string! \013 \010

and

    \AThis is a
    setup string! \013
    \010

The printer output would be the words "This is a setup string" printed on one line. The print head would then be returned to the left margin and the paper advanced one line.

Setup files may be incorporated into batch files to improve your efficiency and to reduce typing errors in the command line of LP. For example, a program source code file that contains lines of more than 80 characters per line could be printed out using CODE.BAT, which contains the setup string show:

\132	(change to compressed print mode)
\s2	(double space the lines)
\n	(number the lines)
\HEADER2	(print the header (identification) on each page and include the filename and timestamp)
\p	(print page numbers)

Note that comment lines are not supported within the setup file!

With this batch file available, the source code file PROGRAM.SRE could be printed using the command line:

    LP program /set:code

Drive designations would be added as necessary, as would pathnames where appropriate.

Warning: WordStar uses the eighth bit of each character byte for its own purposes. This makes it incompatible with the IBM Extended Character Set. *Do not use* the /EXT switch when LP is making a hard copy of a WordStar document.

Norton Change Directory

Version 4.0 Directory Name   **NCD.EXE**

NCD is a new utility program in Version 4.0 and the Advanced Edition. It provides two very useful features. First, it draws a graphic tree structure of the directories in the drive specified. Second, it allows movement directly from one directory to another, regardless of the path changes. This speeds task accomplishment considerably by removing the necessity of inputting the entire path to reach a specific directory.

Format: NCD [*d:*] [*options*] [/R]

Here are the command-line options:

d:	Specify the drive for NCD to read.
MD *directoryname*	Make a directory named *directoryname*.
RD *directoryname*	Remove the directory named *directoryname*.
directoryname	Go to the directory named *directoryname*.
/R	Reread the directory and rebuild the FILEINFO.FI created when NCD was first invoked or last updated by using the /R switch. This option is only needed if a directory or subdirectory has been created or deleted without using NCD.

The first time NCD is invoked, it reads the directory structure of a disk and writes the file TREEINFO.NCD. Every time after that, NCD reads only TREEINFO.NCD before displaying the directory tree structure, making, removing, or changing to the directory entered on the command line. This means that subsequent calls normally will execute much more rapidly than the first one, or when the /R switch is used.

Entering NCD *directoryname* at the prompt will change the disk directory directly. There is no need to enter the full path from the root directory to the directory desired. This means there are fewer keystrokes needed to get to the directory and consequently fewer chances to err. It also means that the full path name does not have to be committed to memory.

Figure 2-41 illustrates the output of the TREE utility of MS-DOS. It shows all 41 of the directories created for this illustration. To access the files of subdirectory 5SUB1 in directory DELTA, the following DOS command would be necessary:

CD \DELTA\7DIR\SUB9\2SUB7\3SUB4\4SUB1\5SUB1

Using NCD, however, the following command would obtain the same result:

NCD 5sub1

There are two directories with the same name on this disk. NCD will move to the first one it finds (the sub of DELTA). If this is not

```
DIRECTORY PATH LISTING
Path: \UTIL
Sub-directories:    NU
                    PCT
                    ARC
                    METRO
                    QD2
Path: \UTIL\NU
Sub-directories:    None
Path: \UTIL\PCT
Sub-directories:    None
Path: \UTIL\ARC
Sub-directories:    None
Path: \UTIL\METRO
Sub-directories:    None
Path: \UTIL\QD2
Sub-directories:    None
Path: \DOS
Sub-directories:    None
Path: \EW
Sub-directories:    BKNU
Path: \EW\BKNU
Sub-directories:    None
Path: \GAME
Sub-directories:    None
```

Fig. 2-41. List of directories as displayed by the TREE utility distributed with MS/PC-DOS. (The display has been compressed vertically.)

the one being sought, enter the same command again and NCD will move to the next subdirectory with that name. To prevent this type of problem, use unique names for each directory. This same logic applies to filenames.

Entering "NCD" with no options results in a graphic display of the directory structure of the disk directories (Fig. 2-42). When this structure is extensive, NCD does not attempt to compress everything into a single screen display. An indication that a structure is larger than the display is the presence of arrowheads at the boundaries of the display (Fig. 2-43). There are more directories along the ANOTH-ER∖SUB path and along the ALPHA = BETA = CHARLIE path.

Using the cursor control arrows to move the reverse video block to the right, along the ADDED directory path, builds the equivalent DOS path in the small window along the bottom of the display (Fig. 2-44). Using the Home key will return the reverse video block to root directory. Pressing the End key will move the reverse video block to the lowest level subdirectory present on that disk.

Without the information portion of the window, it would be possible to display the entire vertical structure of this tree in one screen. Since there is still room on this disk for additional directories, NCD displays a fixed amount of information. The arrowheads now indicate that additional information is above and to the right of this display. By compressing the horizontal space between directory names it might also be possible to display this six-level directory tree in a single screen (Fig. 2-45).

Fig. 2-42. The directory list from Fig. 2-41, displayed with the NCD utility.

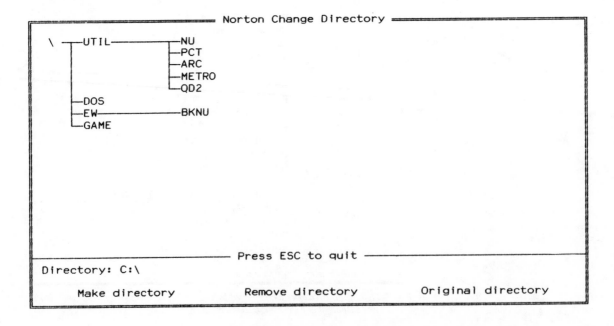

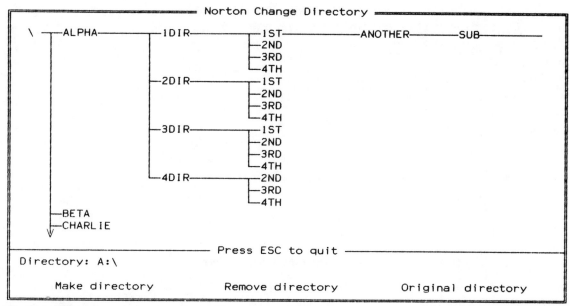

Fig. 2-43. *The initial portion of an NCD tree display, using a directory structure created expressly for these illustrations.*

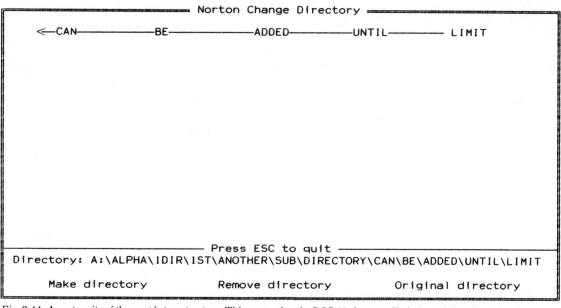

Fig. 2-44. *An extremity of the sample tree structure. This approaches the DOS 63-character limit for a full path name.*

DOS limits a complete path to 63 characters, including the back slashes. NCD does not change this restriction; it just makes it easier to use it.

There is still an eight-character limit on directory names. And it is possible to construct a directory tree beyond the capabilities of the DOS TREE utility that NCD still will be able to manage.

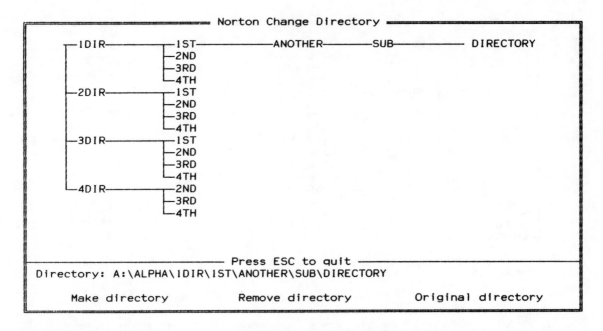

```
══════════════════════════ Norton Change Directory ══════════════════════════
  ┌─1DIR────────────┬─1ST──────────────ANOTHER──────────SUB───────────── DIRECTORY
  │                 ├─2ND
  │                 ├─3RD
  │                 └─4TH
  ├─2DIR────────────┬─1ST
  │                 ├─2ND
  │                 ├─3RD
  │                 └─4TH
  ├─3DIR────────────┬─1ST
  │                 ├─2ND
  │                 ├─3RD
  │                 └─4TH
  └─4DIR────────────┬─2ND
                    ├─3RD
                    └─4TH



  ──────────────────────── Press ESC to quit ────────────────────────
  Directory: A:\ALPHA\1DIR\1ST\ANOTHER\SUB\DIRECTORY

       Make directory           Remove directory          Original directory
```

Fig. 2-45. An intermediate NCD tree display. Notice the change in the path description.

Another difference you'll notice quickly when using NCD is the ability to return to the last directory you were in. NCD "remembers" where you were last; by using the "O"riginal switch (i.e., pressing the "O" key), it will return you there. In case you forget which directory that is, NCD highlights that directory name when the graphic display is on the screen.

Cursor movements within the graphic display are controlled by the arrow keys and the PgUp and PgDn keys. The arrow keys move one directory at a time, while the Pg keys move a screen at a time. The Home key will return you to the root directory and the End key will take you to the lowest level subdirectory in the tree.

Like DOS, NCD requires a directory to be empty before it can be deleted. Unlike DOS, you can recover from a mistake. NCD cannot recover the directory name for you, but the UD (Undelete Directory) program can. Just remember not to write to that disk before attempting to recover the directory. This holds true for the QU (Quick UnErase) and NU (Norton Utility) programs also. Only partial recoveries are possible after DOS has overwritten the sector(s) of an erased (deleted) file or directory. Pressing the Return key will move you directly to the directory in the reverse video block.

Norton Integrator

Version 4.0 Directory Name   NI.EXE

NI, a new addition to the Norton Utilities, is a convenience program. It is not necessarily one of those that you might be willing to give up dessert for a week just to get, but it does accomplish two useful functions. First, it uses a menu display that gives both the two-letter abbreviation for the program and the full name of all 24 Norton Utilities (Fig. 2-46). This takes up the left-hand third of the screen. The other two-thirds of the screen displays a short help file on the utility selected. The information provided on the screen is not as complete as the manual, but it more than suffices as a quick refresher once you know the programs. NI thus is useful for both the frequent and the infrequent user; it provides a reminder of the available switches along with the complete listing of the utility program names. Pressing the F1 key calls up a help screen for NI itself (Fig. 2-47).

If you know which utility you want, the "Speed Search" feature is available by pressing the Tab key. (This is a new feature with Version 4 and the Advanced Edition.) Rather than using the arrow keys to move the reverse video block to your selection, press the Tab key and then enter the first and second letter of the utility you want to run. If the first letter is unique, as it is for Beep, UnRemove Directory and Volume Label, only the first letter is necessary.

Format: NI

Both the Home and End keys are active for quickly moving to either end of the program listing (Fig. 2-46). The cursor is located after the utility name. This allows you to enter the rest of the parameters (pathname, etc.) needed to run the selected file. Pressing the Return key will execute the command.

To edit the command you have entered, the following WordStar-

```
╔══════════════════ The Norton Utilites Integrator ═══════════════════╗
║ ASK                          │                                        ║
║ BEEP                         │ Disk Test      DT [d:] [filespec] [switches] ║
║ DS   Directory Sort          │   Test a disk or file for physical error, move ║
║ *DT* Disk Test               │   questionable clusters, manually mark clusters. ║
║ FA   File Attributes         │   Use DOS' Chkdsk to check for logical errors. ║
║ FF   File Find               │                                        ║
║ FI   File Info               │ DT                                     ║
║ FR   Format Recover          │   Run a Disk Test on the default drive. ║
║ FS   File Size               │ DT maybe.bad /M                        ║
║ LD   List Directories        │   Check maybe.bad, and relocate doubtful clus- ║
║ LP   Line Print              │   ters. (DT won't relocate clusters without /M). ║
║ NCD  Norton CD               │                                        ║
║ NU   Norton Utility          │ Switches                               ║
║ QU   Quick UnErase           │   /B   Perform both a disk test and a file test ║
║ SA   Screen Attributes       │   /Cn  Mark Cluster n as bad           ║
║ SD   Speed Disk              │   /Cn- Mark Cluster n as good; opposite of above ║
║ SI   System Information      │   /D   Test entire Disk                ║
║ TM   Time Mark               │   /F   Test files only.                ║
║ TS   Text Search             │   /LOG Format output for printer or file LOGging ║
║ UD   UnRemove Directory      │   /M   Move doubtful clusters to a safe location ║
║               more...        │   /S   Test subdirectories also        ║
╟──────────────────────────────┴────────────────────────────────────────╢
║  DT                                                                     ║
╚══════════════════════════════════════════════════ Press F1 for Help ═══╝
```

Fig. 2-46. The Norton Integrator menu with Disk Test selected.

```
╔═══════════════════════ The Norton Integrator ════════════════════════╗
║                                                                        ║
║   You can execute any of the Norton Utilities from within NI: Move the ║
║   highlight to the command, type any arguments (optional), and press   ║
║   Enter.                                                               ║
║                                                                        ║
║   Tab              Erase command line and enter Speed Search mode       ║
║   Enter            Run the program on the command line                  ║
║   Space            Leave Speed Search                                   ║
║   Up, Down         Move to previous or next command                     ║
║   Letters          Type arguments on the command line                   ║
║   Esc, F10         Quit NI                                              ║
║                                                                        ║
║ ───────────────────────────── Comments ─────────────────────────────── ║
║                                                                        ║
║   Speed Search     Typing letters moves the highlight to the first      ║
║                    program that matches the letters typed so far.       ║
║                    Press Enter to run the command, or Space to add      ║
║                    arguments.                                           ║
║                                                                        ║
║   [argument]       In the help screens, arguments in brackets are optional ║
║                                                                        ║
║                    Press any key to continue...                         ║
╚════════════════════════════════════════════════════════════════════════╝
```

Fig. 2-47. The help screen for the NI utility itself, called by pressing the F1 key.

compatible commands may be used:

Ctrl-F	Cursor right one word
Ctrl-Right Arrow	Cursor right one word
Ctrl-A	Cursor left one word

[Ctrl-Left Arrow]	Cursor left one word
[Ctrl-Home]	Cursor to the beginning of the line
[Ctrl-End]	Cursor to the end of the line
[Right Arrow]	Cursor right one character
[Ctrl-D]	Cursor right one character
[Left Arrow]	Cursor left one character
[Ctrl-S]	Cursor left one character
[Backspace]	Delete character left
[Del]	Delete character under cursor
[Ctrl-G]	Delete character under cursor
[Ctrl-T]	Delete word right
[Ctrl-W]	Delete word left
[Ctrl-Y]	Delete parameters
[Tab]	Delete the entire line and enter the Speed Search feature

Of the above, only the Tab key will delete the utility file name. Use Ctrl-Home or Ctrl-End to move the command line cursor.

NI also has a circular buffer. This buffer keeps a listing of the commands that have been previously used and can be displayed for reuse. Press Ctrl-E (to move backward) or Ctrl-X (to move forward).

NI calls DOS to run the various programs; therefore, the rules for using DOS (pathnames, filenames, etc.) must be observed when entering information on the command line.

The NI selection screen is redisplayed after running each utility. To exit NI, press the Esc key. This feature permits you to perform all of the tasks necessary to complete work on a disk or project.

Note, too, that NI is one way to be able to access all of the Norton Utilities from within an ASK menu.

Why put a half-screen help file into NI?

I'm not sure why Peter did it because I didn't ask. I do thank him for it because it saves me time. Like many users I know, I read the instructions only when all else fails. The help contained in NI makes referring to the book less necessary.

When would it seem more logical to use the arrow keys to move the cursor, rather than the Speed Search feature?

In a very large directory, you could use Speed Search to move the cursor to a block of similarly named files, then use the cursor keys to select the individual file.

Is there any difference in the way these utilities run on a hard disk versus a floppy?

The only difference I've noticed is the speed. The typical 65-milliseconds hard disk access is much quicker than floppy disk access. There is also a lot less disk swapping.

Is there any way to set up a disk so that NI is always the first utility run?

Yes. On a floppy, a .BAT file can be added to your working copy of the Norton Utilities to run NI first every time. This will give you access to all of the utilities, since both NU and QU are on a separate disk. On a hard disk the same technique will give you access to all of the programs.

Norton Utility

SHORT Directory Name	NU.COM
LONG Directory Name	NORTON.COM
Version 4.0 Directory Name	NU.EXE

NU is the heart of the Norton Utilities. This one program that, when it is "really" needed, is worth the price of the entire package of programs. With the enhancements that have been made over the years, it continues to be a leader in the genre. Note, however, that this program also has the ability to completely destroy your access to any disk. Taking care and following instructions are almost mandatory. The screen displays and the help screens will be useful only to those who take time to *read* them. Along with the format changes in the screens themselves, Version 4.0 and the Advanced Edition have on-line help screens.

Screen displays from more than one version will only be reprinted here when the changes are significant.

Format: NU [*d:*] [*options*] (Version 3.0)

NU [*d:*] [*screen-driver*] [/NOCOLOR] [/ TV] (Version 3.1)

NU [*drive/path/filename*] [*switches*]   (Version 4.0/AE)

The following command-line options and switches are available:

d:	Indicates which drive holds the disk where NU is to work.
/D*n*	Screen driver options switch. Use *n = v* (the default screen driver) for IBM PCs and "fully" compatibles. Use *n* = 1 with BIOS-compatible machines, or *n* = 2 with other MS-DOS machines that are not BIOS-compatible (the latter requires ANSI.SYS). Note also that using the /D2 option and the Advanced Edition, absolute sectors are not accessible.
/NOCOLOR	The Version 3.0 no color (monochrome) option.
/NOC	The no color or monochrome option in Version 3.1.

/TV	Makes special adjustments so that NU can work with IBM's TopView program.
/F*n* /B*n*	Color control options available in Version 3.1. An *n* value of 0 to 15 permits the direct selection of a specific color.
[Alt-F3]	Foreground color control. Successively pressing this key will cycle the screen through each of the 16 available colors. Version 4.0 and AE.
[Alt-F4]	Background color control. The color values for the numbers 0 thru 15 are those listed in the BASIC manual. Version 4.0 and AE.
/BW[Alt-F1]	Indicates that NU is running on a monochrome composite monitor from a CGA card. Version 4.0 and AE.
/P	The display-printable-character option. This becomes useful when trying to use PRNTSCR to get a hardcopy of the display. Version 3.1.
[Alt-F2]	This key combination is available to toggle the IBM graphics character set on and off from within the NU program. This can be very useful when trying to print out hex data. Version 4.0 and AE.
/EBCDIC	The Extended Binary Coded Decimal Interchange Code used by IBM mainframe computers. This option allows NU to read and write this code without attempting to display the many nonprintable characters. Version 3.1.
[Alt-F5]	Performs the same function as the /EBCDIC switch and is available from within the NU program. Version 4.0 and AE.
/EUR	Allows for the printing of the European character set. Version 3.1.
/EXT [Alt-F6]	Allows NU to display the IBM Extended Character Set (above ASCII 127). The Alt-F6 key combination can be used as a toggle from within the NU program. Version 4.0 and AE.
/M	Maintenance mode (available in the Advanced Edition only); bypasses the DOS logical organization, which you may need to do when working with badly damaged disks.

NU has always been a powerful utility for programmers and "hackers." The Advanced Edition version is now even more powerful. This means that it has the potential to be both much more useful and much more dangerous. With its new editing capabilities, NU can make or break your entire week—instead of just your day—almost instantly.

The value of good housekeeping practices, such as regular hardware maintenance and proper backing up and storage of floppy disks and tapes, cannot be overstressed. Having the power of QU (Quick UnErase) and NU (Norton Utility) never justifies poor operating techniques.

Specifying a filename on the command line, when invoking NU, positions it at the Explore Disk level. Beginning a filename with a question mark (?) brings NU up to the UnErase feature with that file selected.

Access to disks with damaged directories is possible using the "maintenance mode" (/M) switch in the Advanced Edition. In this mode, clusters and sectors, or absolute sectors using an IBM or compatible system, are addressable; files are not. The UnErase feature, a file-oriented routine, is not usable in the maintenance mode.

Making selections on the various menus is done either by pressing the Up Arrow or Down Arrow to position the reverse video block and then pressing the Return key, or by pressing the letter key corresponding to the highlighted capital letter. Pressing the letter key causes NU to run that selection immediately; it is not necessary to press the Return key. This similar to pressing the function keys with earlier versions.

NU positions the reverse video block over the most likely response each time a new menu screen displays. This means that many tasks can be addressed by pressing Return a few times in succession.

Help is available in two forms throughout NU. There are one-line comments on each menu, displayed as the reverse video block from selection to selection, and there are help screens available by pressing F1. The F1 help screens are full-screen displays that are context-sensitive. This means that the screen display is about the selection highlighted by the reverse video block. One other type of "help" is also available—the F9 key. This is the "undo" key.

There are two ways to quit NU. Pressing the F10 key quits immediately and goes to the DOS prompt. Pressing the Esc key backs you out of NU one menu at a time. In either case, you will be warned to complete any unfinished tasks before quitting NU.

What will the Disk Information portion of the NU program tell me?

There are two different pieces of information available. The Map

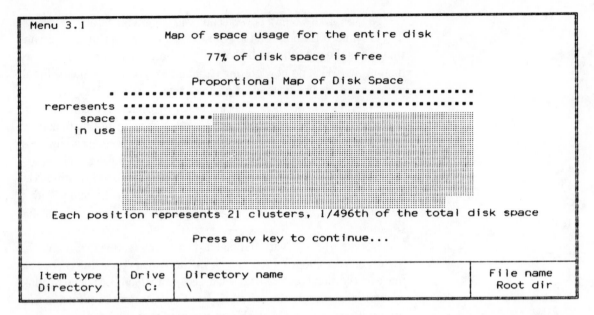

```
 ┌──────────────────────────────────────────────────────────────────────┐
 │ Menu 3.1              Map of space usage for the entire disk           │
 │                                                                        │
 │                         77% of disk space is free                      │
 │                                                                        │
 │                      Proportional Map of Disk Space                    │
 │                   • ••••••••••••••••••••••••••••••••••••••••••          │
 │      represents   • ••••••••••••••••••••••••••••••••••••••••••          │
 │          space    • •••••••••••••                                      │
 │        in use                                                          │
 │                                                                        │
 │                                                                        │
 │                                                                        │
 │                                                                        │
 │      Each position represents 21 clusters, 1/496th of the total disk space │
 │                                                                        │
 │                        Press any key to continue...                    │
 │                                                                        │
 ├─────────────────┬───────────┬──────────────────────────┬──────────────┤
 │  Item type      │ Drive     │ Directory name           │  File name    │
 │  Directory      │  C:       │ \                        │  Root dir     │
 └─────────────────┴───────────┴──────────────────────────┴──────────────┘
```

Fig. 2-48. Menu 3.1 of the main NU program, showing the disk map. (This disk has just been cleaned up with Speed Disk.)

Disk selection (Fig. 2-48) displays a graphic representation of where things are on the disk. This picture is similar to the one that is displayed by the SD (Speed Disk) utility. The two main differences in the displays are the value of each of the "in use" blocks and the fact that this display is static. This means that you are not able to edit or change any of the information shown on this screen directly. The fixed "X" blocks and the bad "B" blocks are included in both displays.

The Technical Information (Fig. 2-49) selection provides a text display which describes the capacity and logical organization of the disk. This selection is about the only way to determine the format's cluster size (number of 512-byte sectors in the cluster). Older versions of DOS formatted in 8-sector clusters (4K bytes); DOS 3.*x* formats in 4-sector clusters (2K bytes).

The most noticeable difference you will see from this change is the reduction in slack or empty space on your hard disk when the majority of your files are relatively small. For example; a file of 5500 bytes occupies a total of 11 sectors (actual). Under DOS 2.*x*, a total of 16 sectors or 2 clusters are assigned to that file. With DOS 3.*x*, however, only 12 sectors or 3 clusters are assigned to that file. Although the number of clusters assigned has increased, the actual amount of disk space assigned has decreased by 4 sectors (2K bytes). This means that these 4 sectors (1 cluster) can be assigned to another file.

The last line says that the root directory can only hold 512 files. Am I limited to 512 files on my hard disk?

No, the limit is on the root directory, not the hard disk. You may not have more than 512 *files* in the root directory, but you may have any number of subdirectories. These files are not a part of the root directory and therefore are not included in the 512-file total. This means that the actual total number of files will be limited to the disk space available.

I've noticed a file called NU.HLP on the disk. What does it do?

This file is not one of the Norton Utilities. It is a file which is called by NU when you press the F1 key at any of the screens. There are a number of helpful hints on these screens. The first one (Fig. 2-50) gives you a bit more information about the selections that are available. The bottom half of the screen lists the various "hot" keys that are active.

The Explore Disk helps screen (Fig. 2-51) provides a more complete explanation of the information which displays along the bottom of the various NU screens. These bottom two lines and the top line of the NU screens will normally provide you with a complete description of your location on the disk.

When you are choosing items to work on or just investigate, the help screen in Fig. 2-52 will give you more information about what the selections mean. Also provided are the locations and/or means for finding some specific areas. Access to the Partition Table is limited to users of the Advanced Edition of the Norton Utilities. The rest

Fig. 2-49. NU menu 3.2 (Technical Information), displaying information for the disk used in Fig. 2-48.

```
Menu 3.2
                           Technical Information

          Drive C:

          Basic storage capacity:
              21 million characters (megabytes)
              77% of disk space is free

          Logical dimensions:
              Sectors are made up of 512 bytes
              Tracks are made up of 17 sectors per disk side
              There are 4 disk sides
              The disk space is made up of 614 cylinders
              Space for files is allocated in clusters of 4 sectors
              There are 10,405 clusters
              Each cluster is 2,048 bytes
              The disk's root directory can hold 512 files



                    Press any key to continue...
```

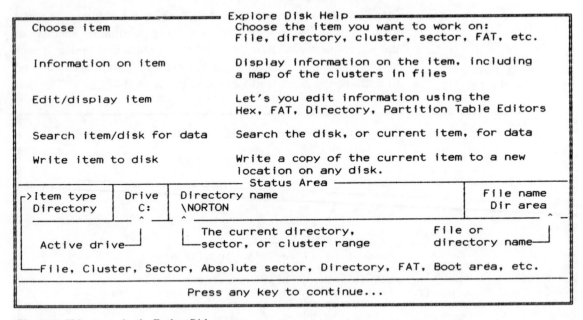

```
================ Main Menu Help ================

  Explore Disk           View or edit data
                         Edit FAT, Directory, Hex, and Partition Table
                         Search for data
                         View information on item
                         Copy data from one area of disk to another

  Unerase                Recover lost or erased files

  Disk information       Map disk usage
                         Report technical information on your disk
  _____ Keys _____

  Esc                    Back-up to the previous menu
  F10                    Exit to DOS
  Enter                  Select a menu item
  Up arrow               Move highlight up
  Down arrow             Move highlight down
  letter                 You can select a menu by typing the letter shown
                         in bright, such as the D in "Disk information"


                     Press any key to continue...
```

Fig. 2-50. *Help screen accessed from the main menu of NU by pressing the F1 key.*

```
================ Explore Disk Help ================

  Choose item              Choose the item you want to work on:
                           File, directory, cluster, sector, FAT, etc.

  Information on item      Display information on the item, including
                           a map of the clusters in files

  Edit/display item        Let's you edit information using the
                           Hex, FAT, Directory, Partition Table Editors

  Search item/disk for data  Search the disk, or current item, for data

  Write item to disk       Write a copy of the current item to a new
                           location on any disk.
  _____ Status Area _____
  ->Item type  | Drive |  Directory name           |    File name
    Directory  |  C:   |  \NORTON                   |    Dir area
            ^    ^          ^                              ^
    Active drive-┘      ┌─ The current directory,      File or
                        └─ sector, or cluster range    directory name─┘

  ─File, Cluster, Sector, Absolute sector, Directory, FAT, Boot area, etc.

                     Press any key to continue...
```

Fig. 2-51. *Help screen for the Explore Disk menu.*

of us will just have to look at the illustrations and imagine.

The keys used to move around the screen and the active "F" keys are displayed on the help screen in Fig. 2-53. Again, only Advanced Edition users will have access to the directory, FAT and Partition

```
╔══════════════════════ Choose Item Help ══════════════════════╗
║  Change drive           To select an item from another disk    ║
║                                                                 ║
║  change Directory       Change to another directory using a visual tree ║
║                                                                 ║
║  File                   Select file or directory clusters (from the     ║
║                         current directory)                      ║
║                                                                 ║
║  cLuster                Select a single or range of clusters    ║
║                                                                 ║
║  Sector                 Select a single or range of sectors     ║
║                                                                 ║
║  Absolute sector        Select a single or range of absolute sectors    ║
║                                                                 ║
║  ──────────────────── Choosing special items ────────────────── ║
║                                                                 ║
║  Dir area               Choose the "Dir area" pseudo-file       ║
║                                                                 ║
║  FAT and Boot areas     Change to the root directory ( \ ) and choose    ║
║                         the pseudo-files FAT area or Boot area  ║
║                                                                 ║
║  Partition Table        Select Absolute sector Side 0, Cylinder 0, Sector 1 ║
║                                                                 ║
║                         Press any key to continue...            ║
╚═════════════════════════════════════════════════════════════════╝
```

Fig. 2-52. Help screen for the Choose Item menu.

```
╔═══════════════════════ Directory Editor Help ═══════════════════════╗
║                                                                      ║
║   Enter, Esc          Save (or discard) your editing changes         ║
║   Tab, Shift-Tab      Move to next or previous field                 ║
║   Space               Toggle attributes or am-pm                     ║
║   F9                  Undo changes to the entry under the cursor      ║
║   Cursor keys         Move the cursor through the data               ║
║   PgDn, PgUp          Move to the next or previous screen            ║
║   Home, End           Move to the first or last entry in the directory║
║                                                                      ║
║  ─────────────────────── Function Keys ─────────────────────────── ║
║                                                                      ║
║                                          Advanced Edition only       ║
║                                                                      ║
║   F1     Display this help screen     F4     Directory Editor        ║
║   F2     Hex Editor                   F5     FAT Editor              ║
║   F3     Text display                 F6     Partition Table Editor  ║
║                                                                      ║
║                    Press any key to continue...                      ║
╚══════════════════════════════════════════════════════════════════════╝
```

Fig. 2-53. Help screen for the File or Directory Select menu.

Table in the edit mode. Since backups *before* trying to edit are so necessary, this additional reminder is included.

The Hex Editor (Fig. 2-54) will be the most-used editor. With it, all of the information in the data areas may be changed. This includes

```
╔═══════════════════════ Hex Editor Help ═══════════════════════╗
║                                                                ║
║     Enter, Esc         Save (or discard) your editing changes  ║
║     Tab                Switch between Hex (left) and ASCII (right) windows ║
║     Backspace          Undo changes to the byte under the cursor ║
║     Cursor keys        Move the cursor through the data         ║
║     PgDn, PgUp         Move to the next or previous page of data ║
║     Home, End          Move to the first or last page in the item ║
║                                                                ║
║                              Advanced Edition only             ║
║                                                                ║
║     F1         Display this help screen    F4      Directory Editor ║
║     F2         Hex Editor                  F5      FAT Editor   ║
║     F3         Text display                F6      Partition Table Editor ║
║                                                                ║
║ ──────────── FAT or Partition Table Editing (AE only) ──────────── ║
║                                                                ║
║     FAT                Under Choose item, select the FAT area   ║
║                        pseudo-file from the root directory ( \ ) ║
║                                                                ║
║     Partition Table    Under Choose item, select the Absolute sector ║
║                        Side 0, Cylinder 0, Sector 1            ║
║                                                                ║
║                        Press any key to continue...            ║
║                                                                ║
╚════════════════════════════════════════════════════════════════╝
```

the ability to edit the code of compiled programs and the header information on various other types of files.

Fig. 2-54. Help screen displayed while a file is being processed with the hex editor.

If you are very careful, and have lots of time to try the exercise, it is possible to manually write an entire file to the disk using the editor in NU. This would include the directory listing, FAT information, and the data in the appropriate clusters. For a text file, it obviously would be faster and easier to use the text editor. Either way, the idea comes through that NU gives you access to everything.

Quick UnErase

SHORT Directory Name	**QU.COM**
LONG Directory Name	**QUNERASE.COM**
Version 4.0 Directory Name	**QU.EXE**

QU program is a streamlined version of the UnErase feature which is the heart of the main NU program. While it does not contain all of the NU features, it has an automatic mode which permits goof-proof recoveries of many newly deleted files.

Format: QU [*d*:] [*path/filename*] [/A]

The command-line options are:

_d:_   The drive designation where the file is to be found.

path/filename   The location on the specified or default drive where the file is to be found. QU defaults to *.* if no filename is specified. The wildcard characters * and ? may be used in the specification.

/A   Tells QU to go about its attempt automatically. This means there is no user input required. QU locates the file(s) and supplies a first letter that will give the file a unique filename. Later, using the DOS REName routine, you can convert that name to the proper name for the file(s) recovered.

Using QU in the interactive mode means that you will be asked to supply a first letter for each filename that QU is able to recover. Shown in Fig. 2-55 is a representative screen captured from an interactive QU session. The lines marked with asterisks (*) normally are overwritten on the screen. They have been shown here for your information.

With Version 4.0 and the Advanced Edition, the format changes somewhat. Without duplicating too much of the information, Fig. 2-56 shows an example of the new display.

QU works on both hard and floppy disks. It will work faster on smaller directories, such as those on a floppy disk. QU will only re-

```
A>QU

QU-Quick UnErase. Version 3.10. (C) Copr 1984-86. Peter Norton

    There are 2 erased files in this directory
    1 of them may possibly be Quick-UnErased

    Erased files lose the first character of their names
    After selecting each file to Quick-UnErase, you will be
    asked to supply the missing character

    ?L.COM          4,536 bytes   3:10 pm  Fri Nov  1 85
*Do you wish to Quick-UnErase this file (Y/N) ? y
*What is the first character of ?L.COM ? v
*The filename 'VL.COM' will be used for the new Quick-UnErased file

    ?EAD.ME.BAT     1,060 bytes   3:10 pm  Fri Nov  1 85
It is not possible to Quick-UnErase this file
Its data space is being used by another file
Press and key to continue
```

Fig. 2-55. Typical screen from a Quick UnErase session in interactive mode.

```
A>qu b:*.com

QU-Quick UnErase, Advanced Edition, (C) Copr 1987, Peter Norton

Directory of B:\
    Erased file specification: *.COM
    Number of erased files: 8
    Number that can be Quick-UnErased: 8

    Erased files lose the first character of their names.
    After selectiong each file to Quick-UnErase, you will be
    asked to supply the missing character

    ?ndersb.com       10 bytes    7:41 pm  Tue Sep 25 84

Quick-UnErase this file (Y/N) ? Y

* Enter the first character of the filename: U
* 'undersb.com' Quick-UnErased
    ?clock.com       512 bytes    6:43 pm  Mon Jan  5 87

Quick- . . . .
```

Fig. 2-56. Quick UnErase format in Version 4.0 and the Advanced Edition.

cover complete files. NU must be used if an attempt is to be made on a partial file. If the attempt to recover a file with QU is not successful, delete the attempt and try again with NU. Figure 2-57 shows a typical screen representation for an automatic QU session.

Notice that QU is file-oriented. Its speed and value are best seen when trying to recover a file that has just been (accidentally) deleted. CHKDSK/F, DT, and NU provide other means of recovering data accidentally deleted or damaged. The capabilities of the Norton Utilities programs DT and NU each have their own section elsewhere in this book. Some use of the DOS utility CHKDSK program is covered in the section on DT.

By using the FA (File Attributes) utility program to make especially valuable files "read-only," some additional safety can be included.

What does it mean when QU reports that a file is cross-linked?

Cross linking means that two or more files are claiming that the same sector is a valid data location. This happens when new files are written to disks which contain deleted files. It can also happen if an existing file is modified on a disk with other deleted files on it. This is a very good reason to do file recovery before attempting to add to or modify the files on that disk.

Is there any way to prevent cross linking?

Fig. 2-57. Screen representation of an automatic QU session.

Yes, WIPEFILE can be used to delete a file. This will ensure

```
A>qu /a

QU-Quick-UnErase, Version 3.10, (C) Copr 1984-86, Peter Norton

    There are 3 erased files in this directory
    2 of them may possibly be Quick-UnErased

    Erased files lose the first character of their names
    Quick-UnErase will automatically replace them

    ?D.COM          10,400 bytes   3:10 pm  Fri Nov  1 85
The filename 'AD.COM' will be used for the new Quick-UnErased file
    ?L.COM           4,536 bytes   3:10 pm  Fri Nov  1 85
The filename 'AL.COM' will be used for the new Quick-UnErased file

    ?EADME.BAT       1,060 bytes   3:10 pm  Fri Nov  1 85
It is not possible to Quick-UnErase this file
Its data space is being used by another program

A>
```

that all of the information about the deleted file is erased. This will also prevent QU and NU from recovering any of the data. The other way is to do all your file recovery first. Then, use WIPEDISK /E to clear all of the free data storage space.

Screen Attributes

SHORT Directory Name	SA.COM
LONG Directory Name	SCRATR.COM
Version 4.0 Directory Name	SA.EXE

Some programs do not support color, even when the system is color-compatible. SA provides a means of adding some color to your session. There is no ability (indeed, no reason) to redirect the output of this utility to the printer or a disk file.

Format: SA [*prefix*] *main-setting* [/N]

SA *main-setting* [/N]

SA [*prefix*] [*foreground*] [ON *background*] [/N]

SA [*intensity*] [*foreground*] [ON *background*] [/N]

The optional *prefix* can specify an *intensity* modifier and/or the BLINKING attribute:

BRIGHT
BOLD
BLINKING

The possible values of *main-setting* are:

NORMAL
REVERSE
UNDERLINE

The value of *foreground* may be set to:

WHITE	BLACK	RED	GREEN
YELLOW	BLUE	MAGENTA	CYAN

The ON *background* may specify:

WHITE	BLACK	RED	GREEN
YELLOW	BLUE	MAGENTA	CYAN

The /N switch inhibits setting a border that matches the background color.

The results you get using SA will depend on the hardware you are using. Your system must be able to display colors, or various shades on your monochrome screen.

Some programs set their own screen attributes. This will not interfere with the operation of SA. Some programs will replace the screen attributes (colors) upon termination, while others do not. Not all computers support all of the options that DOS supports. Experimentation will determine the limits of your system and the more pleasing combinations.

If the utility ANSI.SYS is required for SA to run properly, an error message will prompt you to install it. No harm will be done if you run SA before installing ANSI.SYS. Your DOS manual will explain how to include the command DEVICE = ANSI.SYS in the CONFIG.SYS file.

The /N switch is used by all computers that are not fully IBM-compatible. This is because SA uses IBM-specific means to produce a colored border for the screen. The border will be the same color as the background. The EGA card generates a borderless display. This means there will be no border regardless of the /N switch.

While the final choice of colors is yours, the following combinations have proven useful to many others.

```
SA WHITE ON BLUE
SA YELLOW ON BLUE
SA BLACK ON GREEN
```

Or how about these to attract attention, especially if used with BEEP?

```
SA REVERSE
SA BRIGHT BLINKING RED ON BLUE
```

Illustrations of the various color combinations will have to be provided by your system or that of a friend, if yours does not support color. Peter Norton has used his favorite colors to good advantage within the utilities. Note: The REVERSE video switch may not work on some systems where the display is not fully IBM-compatible. The TI Professional is one of those that does not support the REVERSE switch.

SA may be included in batch files between various programs to restore colors, add color or, in ASK to change the display for specific programs.

Is there any way to check which color combinations look best?

There are two way available. The trial-and-error method and the

```
CLS
SA WHITE on BLACK                              ;_____
PAUSE Evaluate this combination
CLS
SA BRIGHT WHITE on BLACK                        ;_____
PAUSE Evaluate this combination
CLS
SA WHITE on RED                                ;_____
PAUSE Evaluate this combination
CLS
SA BRIGHT WHITE on RED                          ;_____
PAUSE Evaluate this combination
CLS
SA WHITE on MAGENTA                            ;_____
PAUSE Evaluate this combination
CLS
SA BRIGHT WHITE on MAGENTA                      ;_____
PAUSE Evaluate this combination
CLS
SA WHITE on BLUE                               ;_____
PAUSE Evaluate this combination
CLS
SA BRIGHT WHITE on BLUE                          ;_____
PAUSE Evaluate this combination
CLS
SA WHITE on GREEN                              ;_____
PAUSE Evaluate this combination
CLS
SA BRIGHT WHITE on GREEN                        ;_____
PAUSE Evaluate this combination
CLS
SA WHITE ON CYAN                               ;_____
PAUSE Evaluate this combination
CLS
SA BRIGHT WHITE on CYAN                          ;_____
PAUSE Evaluate this combination
CLS
SA WHITE on YELLOW                             ;_____
PAUSE Evaluate this combination
CLS
SA BRIGHT WHITE on YELLOW                        ;_____
PAUSE Evaluate this combination
CLS
SA BLACK on RED                                ;_____
PAUSE Evaluate this combination
CLS
SA BLACK on MAGENTA                            ;_____
PAUSE Evaluate this combination
CLS
SA BLACK on BLUE                               ;_____
PAUSE Evaluate this combination
CLS
SA BLACK on CYAN                               ;_____
PAUSE Evaluate this combination
```

```
CLS
SA BLACK on YELLOW                          ;_____
PAUSE Evaluate this combinatioon
CLS
SA BLACK on WHITE                           ;_____
PAUSE Evaluate this combination
CLS
SA RED on MAGENTA                           ;_____
PAUSE Evaluate this combination
CLS
SA BRIGHT RED on MAGENTA                     ;_____
PAUSE Evaluate this combination
CLS
SA RED on BLUE                              ;_____
PAUSE Evaluate this combination
CLS
SA BRIGHT RED on BLUE                        ;_____
PAUSE Evaluate this combination
CLS
SA RED on GREEN                             ;_____
PAUSE Evaluate this combination
CLS
SA BRIGHT RED on GREEN                       ;_____
PAUSE Evaluate this combination
CLS
SA RED on CYAN                              ;_____
PAUSE Evalluate this combination
CLS
SA BRIGHT RED on CYAN                        ;_____
PAUSE Evaluate this combination
CLS
SA RED on YELLOW                            ;_____
PAUSE Evaluate this combination
CLS
SA BRIGHT RED on YELLOW                      ;_____
PAUSE Evaluate this combination
CLS
SA RED on WHITE                             ;_____
PAUSE Evaluate this combination
CLS
SA BRIGHT RED ON WHITE                       ;_____
PAUSE Evaluate this combination
CLS
SA RED on BLACK                             ;_____
PAUSE Evaluate this combination
CLS
SA BRIGHT RED on BLACK                       ;_____
PAUSE Evaluate this combination
CLS
SA MAGENTA on BLUE                          ;_____
PAUSE Evaluate this combination
CLS
SA BRIGHT MAGENTA on BLUE                    ;_____
PAUSE Evaluate this combination
```

```
CLS
SA MAGENTA on GREEN                    ;_____
PAUSE Evaluate this combination
CLS
SA BRIGHT MAGENTA on GREEN             ;_____
PAUSE Evaluate this combination
CLS
SA MAGENTA on CYAN                     ;_____
PAUSE Evaluate this combination
CLS
SA BRIGHT MAGENTA on CYAN              ;_____
PAUSE Evaluate this combination
CLS
SA MAGENTA on YELLOW                   ;_____
PAUSE Evaluate this combination
CLS
SA BRIGHT MAGENTA on YELLOW            ;_____
PAUSE Evaluate this combination
CLS
SA MAGENTA on WHITE                    ;_____
PAUSE Evaluate this combination
CLS
SA BRIGHT MAGENTA on WHITE             ;_____
PAUSE Evaluate this combination
CLS
SA MAGENTA on BLACK                    ;_____
PAUSE Evaluate this combination
CLS
SA BRIGHT MAGENTA on BLACK             ;_____
PAUSE Evaluate this combination
CLS
SA MAGENTA on RED                      ;_____
PAUSE Evaluate this combination
CLS
SA BRIGHT MAGENTA on RED               ;_____
PAUSE Evaluate this combination
CLS
SA BLUE on GREEN                       ;_____
PAUSE Evaluate this combination
CLS
SA BRIGHT BLUE on GREEN                ;_____
PAUSE Evaluate this combination
CLS
SA BLUE on CYAN                        ;_____
PAUSE Evaluate this combination
CLS
SA BRIGHT BLUE on CYAN                 ;_____
PAUSE Evaluate this combination
CLS
SA BLUE on YELLOW                      ;_____
PAUSE Evaluate this combination
CLS
SA BRIGHT BLUE on YELLOW               ;_____
PAUSE Evaluate this combination
```

```
CLS
SA BLUE on WHITE                      ;_____
PAUSE Evaluate this combination
CLS
SA BRIGHT BLUE on WHITE               ;_____
PAUSE Evaluate this combination
CLS
SA BLUE on BLACK                      ;_____
PAUSE Evaluate this combination
CLS
SA BRIGHT BLUE on BLACK               ;_____
PAUSE Evaluate this combination
CLS
SA BLUE on RED                        ;_____
PAUSE Evaluate this combination
CLS
SA BRIGHT BLUE on RED                 ;_____
PAUSE Evaluate this combination
CLS
SA BLUE on MAGENTA                    ;_____
PAUSE Evaluate this combination
CLS
SA BRIGHT BLUE on MAGENTA             ;_____
PAUSE Evaluate this combination
CLS
SA GREEN on CYAN                      ;_____
PAUSE Evaluate this combination
CLS
SA BRIGHT GREEN on CYAN               ;_____
PAUSE Evaluate this combination
CLS
SA GREEN on YELLOW                    ;_____
PAUSE Evaluate this combination
CLS
SA BRIGHT GREEN on YELLOW             ;_____
PAUSE Evaluate this combination
CLS
SA GREEN on WHITE                     ;_____
PAUSE Evaluate this combination
CLS
SA BRIGHT GREEN on WHITE              ;_____
PAUSE Evaluate this combination
CLS
SA GREEN on BLACK                     ;_____
PAUSE Evaluate this combination
CLS
SA BRIGHT GREEN on BLACK              ;_____
PAUSE Evaluate this combination
CLS
SA GREEN on RED                       ;_____
PAUSE Evaluate this combination
CLS
SA BRIGHT GREEN on RED                ;_____
PAUSE Evaluate this combination
```

```
CLS
SA GREEN on MAGENTA                    ;_____
PAUSE Evaluate this combination
CLS
SA BRIGHT GREEN on MAGENTA             ;_____
PAUSE Evaluate this combination
CLS
SA GREEN on BLUE                       ;_____
PAUSE Evaluate this combination
CLS
SA BRIGHT GREEN on BLUE                ;_____
PAUSE Evaluate this combination
CLS
SA CYAN on YELLOW                      ;_____
PAUSE Evaluate this combination
CLS
SA BRIGHT CYAN on YELLOW               ;_____
PAUSE Evaluate this combination
CLS
SA CYAN on WHITE                       ;_____
PAUSE Evaluate this combination
CLS
SA BRIGHT CYAN on WHITE                ;_____
PAUSE Evaluate this combination
CLS
SA CYAN on BLACK                       ;_____
PAUSE Evaluate this combination
CLS
SA BRIGHT CYAN on BLACK                ;_____
PAUSE Evaluate this combination
CLS
SA CYAN on RED                         ;_____
PAUSE Evaluate this combination
CLS
SA BRIGHT CYAN on RED                  ;_____
PAUSE Evaluate this combination
CLS
SA CYAN on MAGENTA                     ;_____
PAUSE Evaluate this combination
CLS
SA BRIGHT CYAN on MAGENTA              ;_____
PAUSE Evaluate this combination
CLS
SA CYAN on BLUE                        ;_____
PAUSE Evaluate this combination
CLS
SA BRIGHT CYAN on BLUE                 ;_____
PAUSE Evaluate this combination
CLS
SA CYAN on GREEN                       ;_____
PAUSE Evaluate this combination
CLS
SA BRIGHT CYAN on GREEN                ;_____
PAUSE Evaluate this combination
```

```
CLS
SA YELLOW on WHITE                        ;_____
PAUSE Evaluate this combination
CLS
SA BRIGHT YELLOW on WHITE                 ;_____
PAUSE Evaluate this combination
CLS
SA YELLOW on BLACK                        ;_____
PAUSE Evaluate this combination
CLS
SA BRIGHT YELLOW on BLACK                 ;_____
PAUSE Evaluate this combination
CLS
SA YELLOW on RED                          ;_____
PAUSE Evaluate this combination
CLS
SA BRIGHT YELLOW on RED                   ;_____
PAUSE Evaluate this combination
CLS
SA YELLOW on MAGENTA                      ;_____
PAUSE Evaluate this combination
CLS
SA BRIGHT YELLOW on MAGENTA              ;_____
PAUSE Evaluate this combination
CLS
SA YELLOW on BLUE                         ;_____
PAUSE Evaluate this combination
CLS
SA BRIGHT YELLOW on BLUE                  ;_____
PAUSE Evaluate this combination
CLS
SA YELLOW on GREEN                        ;_____
PAUSE Evaluate this combination
CLS
SA BRIGHT YELLOW on GREEN                 ;_____
PAUSE Evaluate this combination
CLS
SA YELLOW on CYAN                         ;_____
PAUSE Evaluate this combination
CLS
SA BRIGHT YELLOW on CYAN                  ;_____
PAUSE Evaluate this combination
SA NORMAL
CLS
```

COLORS.BAT method. Using the trial-and-error method may work, but it may also take longer. Furthermore in order to be sure that all of the possible combinations have been evaluated, you will at least duplicate the work done in the COLORS.BAT file.

COLORS.BAT (Fig. 2-58) is a simple, fixed batch file that can be written to a disk using your favorite ASCII editor. It has few requirements:

1. Boot your system with the ANSI.SYS program installed.
2. Make certain COLORS.BAT and SA (Screen Attributes) are in the same directory or on the same disk.

I have placed a semicolon and a string of underscores (__) after each combination in the printed codefile. These are not required on the disk file. They are there for your use. Record your comments on each combination as it displays. (Some of the combinations are very hard to read.)

BRIGHT and BOLD do the same thing, so only BRIGHT is used. WHITE (as opposed to BRIGHT WHITE) on my monitor looks gray. Most of the other colors are harder to define in the foreground when they are not bright. BRIGHT BLACK is not a valid combination; if you try it, SA displays an error message. For those of you who don't want to do all of this coding, you can omit all the CLS commands and the prompts after the PAUSE commands.

Speed Disk

Advanced Edition Directory Name   **SD.EXE**

SD is a new utility, found only in the Advanced Edition. It does a number of very useful tasks: It reduces to a minimum the wasted space on a disk, it eliminates all file fragments, and it provides a visual indication of what it is doing. Redirection may be used when the REPORT option is used. This will provide a hard copy of the result

WARNING * WARNING * WARNING * WARNING

> SD physically moves file(s) and sector(s) as it operates. This means that memory-resident programs may not be able to locate the program file when SD has done its work. This also means that if the system is interrupted during the operation of the SD program, information may be lost.

> SD may not be compatible with all of the copy protection schemes in use on your disk(s). This is especially true of hard disks. Before running SD the first time, backup the entire hard disk. After verifying compatibility, it should not be necessary to perform this step. Remember to run FR (format recover) after running SD.

Format: SD [*d:*] [/REPORT] [/S]

SD [*d:*] [*path/filename*/REPORT] [/S]

The SD command line options are:

d: The drive designation.

/REPORT   Generates a report and does not make any changes to the files on the disk.

path/filename **/REPORT**   Provides a report on a specific file. Since no changes are made, there is no danger of RAM residents getting lost, or other inconveniences.

/S   Instructs SD to include all subdirectories when rearranging the files.

SD improves disk usage and reduces access times. By relocating the fragmented sectors of a file into a contiguous sector chain, SD reduces read/write head motion during disk accessing. SD also places all directories before all files at the beginning of the disk.

A typical session with SD would look something like Fig. 2-59 and Fig. 2-60. Note the organization of the screen in Fig. 2-59. The cursor sits on the drive letter and blinks. The options are to press Return, Escape, a letter key and then Return, or the arrow keys to reposition the cursor and then the Return key. This allows you to run SD on the disk indicated, exit SD altogether, or change the drive selection and then run SD.

After reading all of the information on the disk, SD begins rearranging it into contiguous sectors of directories and then files. One thing it will not do is move hidden or system files. This prevents problems with some programs that install ''keys'' in certain locations and then must be able to locate them again at the same place. In Fig. 2-60 there is a small system file at the beginning of the disk. There are also some previously identified bad sectors on this disk.

Good operating practice should require that this disk be repaired or discarded. Note that there is a large blank area after the portion of the screen identified as unused space. The disk used has a capacity of 360K bytes. A 20-megabyte hard disk still leaves some blank space available.

Fig. 2-59. Drive selection screen of the Speed Disk utility. (Drive A: had been specified on the command line.)

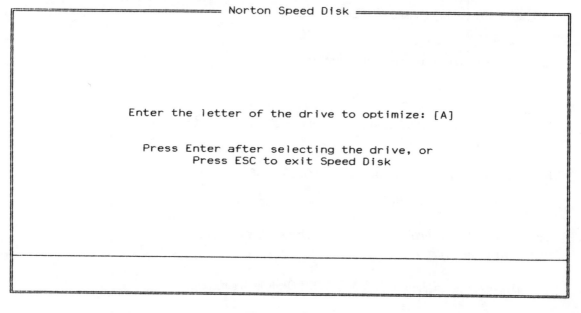

```
══════════ Norton Speed Disk ══════════




        Enter the letter of the drive to optimize: [A]

        Press Enter after selecting the drive, or
              Press ESC to exit Speed Disk



```

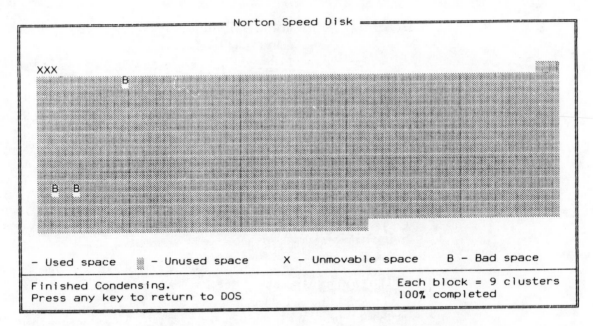

Fig. 2-60. The graphic display after SD runs (Version 4.0 and Advanced Edition).

Continued use of a disk with "marked" bad sectors is not immediately dangerous to data storage. It could indicate a defect in manufacturing, or it could indicate that the disk is getting worn. Since the sectors are marked, DOS will not attempt to write anything to these sectors. I prefer to use these disks for archival purposes to reduce the possibility of data loss.

Can I abort SD at any time without danger?

SD can be aborted safely using Ctrl-C. Aborting by any other means can cause problems.

What types of problems can be caused?

SD relocates files on the disk. If the file is relocated and the new location is not written to the FAT (file allocation table), it will be impossible for DOS to find. Or, if SD is aborted during a write, it may not write the entire file back to the disk.

Will SD work if there are problems with any of the files?

No, SD will report problems and then abort its operation.

After running SD is there any data left in the sectors/clusters that are now empty?

No, SD operates much like WIPEFILE or WIPEDISK in that respect.

How large a disk can SD manipulate?

SD has the same limit as DOS, currently 32 megabytes. As DOS learns to address more space, I expect SD to be able to handle these disks. This 32M limit is a logical limit. This means that a very large disk divided into different lettered drives can be acted upon by SD, one logical drive at a time.

System Information

SHORT Directory Name	**SI.COM**
LONG Directory Name	**SYSINFO.COM**
Version 4.0 Directory Name	**SI.EXE**

SI provides information about your system as a displayed, printed, or filed report. Version 3.1 provides a performance indicator (index) relative to the IBM PC. Version 4.0 (or Advanced Edition) provides this indicator relative to the IBM PC XT.

Format: SI [/N]

SI [*d:*] [*switches*] [> | > >] [*path/filename|device*]

(Version 4.0)

The command-line options and switches are:

/N   Tells SI not to perform an active memory test. This test will cause some not "fully" compatible computers to "hang," requiring that they be rebooted.

/LOG   Tells SI to format the report in a manner suitable for printing or redirecting to a disk file. This is similar to the /T switch used in another utility.

> | > >   DOS operators to redirect or redirect-and-append the program output.

path/filename|device   The location for the new file, the file to be overwritten, the file to receive the append or the device to receive the program output.

The Disk Index (DI) is only calculated for hard disks. The system index (SI) requires the DI for an input; if there is no hard disk in the system, only the processor index (PI) is calculated.

The information reported by SI for a not "fully" compatible system may not be as complete as a fully compatible one. The information reports look similar to those shown in Fig. 2-61 and Fig. 2-62.

Because the /N switch was used, the second (live) memory test was not performed. The live memory test actually goes out and tests the amount of main memory, memory used by screen display adapters, expanded and extended memory, and ROM-BIOS extensions. The latter are the ROMs that are present on some add-on boards. SI will report these under the heading of ROM-BIOS extensions.

Will SI report any increases that a program like "Lightning" might be responsible for?

Yes. If you run SI before installing one of these programs and then again after installation, SI will report the speed increase.

How is the system index (SI) calculated?

It appears to be the mean of the sum of the processor index (PI) and the disk index (DI).

One example showed a TI Professional Computer report. Will SI report just the PI, or can it access the hard disk and calculate the System Index?

Fig. 2-61. System Information report on the TI Professional Computer (Version 4.0 and Advanced Edition).

The TI disk controller is not compatible and does not allow SI to access the TI hard disk. This means that only the processor index will be calculated.

```
           Computer Name:  TI Professional
        Operating System:  DOS 2.11
          Main Processor:  Intel 8088        Serial Ports:  2
            Co-Processor:  None            Parallel Ports:  1
   Video Display Adapter:  Monochrome
      Current Video Mode:  Text, 80 x 25 Monochrome
   Available Disk Drives:  6, A: - F:

DOS reports 512 K-bytes of memory:
    168 K-bytes used by DOS and resident programs
    344 K-bytes available for application programs

  Computing Index (CI), relative to IBM/XT: 1.1
      Disk Index (DI), relative to IBM/XT: Not computed. No drive specified.

Performance Index (PI), relative to IBM/XT: Not computed.
```

```
SI-Systen Information, Advanced Edition, (C) Copr. 1987, Peter Norton

          Copyright Notice:  (C) 1984,1985,1986 PHOENIX TECHNOLOGIES LTD
          Operating System:  DOS 3.30
       Built-in BIOS dated:  Thursday, May 29, 1986
            Main Processor:  NEC V20              Serial Ports:  1
              Co-Processor:  None               Parallel Ports:  1
     Video Display Adapter:  Enhanced Graphics, 256 K-bytes
        Current Video Mode:  Text, 80 x 25 Black and White
      Available Disk Drives:  3, A: - C:

DOS reports 640 K-bytes of memory:
     57 K-bytes used by DOS and resident programs
    583 K-bytes available for application programs
A search for active memory finds:
    640 K-bytes main memory     (at hex 0000-A000)
     32 K-bytes display memory  (at hex B800-C000)
ROM-BIOS Extensions are found at hex paragraphs: C000 C800

     Computing Index (CI), relative to IBM/XT: Testing..3.1
         Disk Index (DI), relative to IBM/XT: Testing..1.4

     Performance Index (PI), relative to IBM/XT: 2.5
```

Are there any really useful purposes to be served by SI, other than proving that "My computer is faster than your computer?

Fig. 2-62. Typical SI report on a "turbo" clone with its 8 MHz. clock rate selected.

The difference in the System Index figures will give you an indication of the difference in time that the system will require to process the same program. In other words, if Lightning changed the SI from 2.5 to 10, a decrease in running time of 50 to 75 percent might not be an unreasonable expectation. Remember that the SI figure is balanced between processor speed and disk access speed. Lightning is a cache program that increases disk access speed but does nothing for the processor speed. You will have to use your own experience and judgment on the value to be placed in the figures, and the changes that various software, firmware, and hardware enhancements actually make in the system operation for you.

Can I expect two systems with the same SI to perform equally?

Only if everything else is equal. CPU chips, available RAM, the ROM-BIOS version, and even the DOS version can be responsible for differences in the total running or processing time.

Time Mark

SHORT Directory Name	**TM.COM**
LONG Directory Name	**TIMEMARK.COM**
Version 4.0 Directory Name	**TM.EXE**

TM provides a way to display the current time, day, and date in an easily readable form; time the duration of an operation automatically; and generate a file which lists the amount of time spent doing various things.

Format: TM [*function*] [*comments*] [*switches*] [*>* | *> >*] [*device* | *drive/path/filename*]

The command-line options for TimeMark are:

Start
Begins a timing function. Unless a /C*n* switch is included in the command line, the C1 timer will be used. It will also reset a counter and begin a new interval if the counter is already in use.

Report
Displays the time interval since the START command was invoked. The timer continues to run. This allows for the progressive timing of a series of operations. This command is new with Version 4.0. It may be used at any time that a display of the elapsed time is needed.

Stop
Ends the timing function. Issuing a START command without first stopping the previous event does not cause a problem. It will reset the C*n* timer to begin timing the new operation. This command is not used beyond Version 3.1.

Comment
Included on the command line with a REPORT command, which attaches the wording of the comment to the elapsed time reported by TM. This option is usually used when the report is directed to a printer or disk file.

/Cn	Selects one of the four available counters. C1 is the default. Each operates independently.
/L	Moves the time display from the upper right corner of the screen to the upper left corner.
/LOG	Formats the output of TM for printing or filing on disk.
/N	Eliminates the time-day-date display and shows only the elapsed time interval. This the option that is a part of the NU (Norton Utility) program. Quitting the program invokes a TM routine which reports, on screen, just how long NU has been in use.
> | > >	The DOS redirect operators. A single "greater than" symbol tells the system to write or overwrite the new information to filename. Two "greater than" symbols tell the system to append or add to an existing filename. If the filename does not exist, the system will create it.
device/drive/path/filename	Tells the system where the redirected information is to go. The device would normally be the system printer. The *drive/path/filename* parameter tells the system where to find or create the file to hold the information being redirected.

TM may not be fully compatible with non-IBM computer systems. The area of memory used is reserved by IBM but may not be reserved by other manufacturers; some programs also may use this area. Some testing may be necessary to ensure that TM will perform when and where required.

Here's a typical use of TM to time the duration of an operation:

```
TM REPORT "Logging onto DELPHI" > >a:sysop.log
```

This command line would add the string within the quotes to the output of TM and add it to the end of the file SYSOP.LOG in Drive A:. An assumption is made here, that a START Cn command has been issued. TM is unable to report time intervals unless the counters are first started. The command

```
TM REPORT "Off DELPHI" > >A:SYSOP.LOG
```

would conclude the session and make the appropriate notation in the .LOG file.

This pair of commands starts another counter operating and makes a note in a different file:

```
TM START /C2/N
TM REPORT "Book Draft"/C2/LOG > > A:WRITING.LOG
```

Using different filenames or just one filename is a matter of personal choice. The concept of creating an accurate record of the time spent and where it was spent is the same. TM with comments can be placed in batch files as a means of simplifying record keeping. NA (Norton ASK) can be used to incorporate many of the useful features of these programs that should be performed on a routine basis.

Text Search

SHORT Directory Name	**TS.COM**
LONG Directory Name	**TEXTSRCH.COM**
Version 4.0 Directory Name	**TS.EXE**

TS started out as a simple search routine which allowed the user to look for strings of characters. These could be letters, words, or punctuation. Its only option was the /N switch. For those of you who "knew it when," TS used to be called SSAR; systems with that utility require EMULATE.COM.

Format: TS (interactive mode)

> TS [*drive/path/filename*] [*search-text*] [*switches*] (automatic mode)

The command-line options for automatic mode are:

drive/path/filename   Searches a specific filename. The wildcard characters ? and * may be used in the filename or extension.

search-text   Specifies the text to be searched for. If the search is for a string of more than one word, it must be enclosed in quotes. TS is not case sensitive, so it does not require you to enter *search-text* exactly as it should be found in the file(s). This also means that you may have a few more matches than anticipated.

/D   Searches the entire disk. The default search area is the data area containing existing files.

/E   Searches only the erased/available space of a disk.

/A   Automates the search by answering "yes" to the questions asked at the various prompts.

/EBCDIC   Tells TS that the file(s) to be searched are in EBCDIC code or are mainframe file(s).

/LOG	Formats the output of TS for printing or writing to a disk file.
/N	Is used for systems that are not fully IBM-compatible and must use the ANSI.SYS driver file.
/WS	Tell TS not to search the ASCII characters between 128 and 255. The default is to search all characters, including the extended character set.
/S	Searches subdirectories.
/T	Sets the non-interactive or Total mode. This provides only a summary of the activities performed by TS.
/C*n*	Start search at cluster *n*.
/EUR	Tells TS, Version 3.1 and later that European language characters may be present in the file(s) to be searched.

When TS matches the text specified in the parameter *search-text*, it highlights it; the method used is IBM-specific. If your system is not fully IBM-compatible, be sure to set the /N switch and be sure that the driver file ANSI.SYS is installed. Failure to follow these recommendations could cause your system to lock. (No damage is done when this happens; it just takes time to start over and do it right the second time.)

Version 3.0 uses only the /N switch to allow TS to search the disks of systems that are not fully IBM-compatible. Many of the functions that are now options external to TS were selectable from within the earlier version.

TS is not limited to searching out the text in ASCII or word processor-type files. It can also search for the cell label of a Lotus spreadsheet or the procedure name of a source code file.

The /WS switch is useful when searches are being conducted in WordStar or other files that use the eighth bit for special purposes. The IBM extended character set (ASCII 128 thru ASCII 255) all have the eighth bit set.

Using the /EBCDIC switch enables the TS translation table to translate ASCII to EBCDIC and the reverse. Using this switch when searching ASCII files will not cause any problems. Not using it during searches of EBCDIC files will invalidate the search.

Even if it is not listed in the manual, the /EUR switch is still available in Version 4.0 and the Advanced Edition. The /A and /T switches serve different purposes. Specifying /A makes a "yes" response for you as if it were an interactive session. The /T switch shows only the filename where matches were found. This means that the text surrounding *search-text* is not shown. One useful combination might be /A/LOG. This will allow you to print or file the search results for use later.

Unless the /LOG switch is used, the output of TS is not suitable for printing or filing. This can be seen very quickly on the screen as the output lines overwrite previously displayed lines. This same type of overwrite occurs at the printer or in a disk file.

When TS is being used in an attempt to recover data, the matching information can be—and should be—written to another drive. This is done by including the drive letter as a part of the filename to which TS is writing. An example of this is:

A:SALFI

(limited by the 8-character limitation of a DOS filename). Should you fill the disk currently in the specified drive, TS will pause and request that a different disk be placed in the drive.

Another way to use TS is to locate missing portions of a file that you are trying to UnErase.

TS completes its tasks faster when the search area is smaller. TS also works faster when searching for only a single word. Searching the whole disk (the /D switch) should not often be necessary. If a search must be conducted outside the active file area, the /E switch will be more useful and faster than the /D switch.

UnRemove Directory

SHORT Directory Name	**UD.COM**
LONG Directory Name	**UNREMDIR.COM**
Version 4.0 Directory Name	**UD.EXE**

UD does for directories what QU does for files.

Format: UD [*d:*] [*pathname*]

The following two command-line options are available:

d: Specifies the drive where the directory is stored.

pathname   Specifies the name of the parent directory of the subdirectory to be unremoved. UD defaults to the current directory when none is specified. UD attempts to recover all of the identifiable directories in the path that have been deleted.

UD does not have the /A switch like the TS program, nor an automatic mode like QU; it operates completely interactively. This means that it will evaluate the undelete possibilities and prompt for a new first letter if recovery is possible.

After recovering the directory name, UD then attempts to recover the contents—the deleted files that were a part of that directory. You can stop UD's search for additional files to UnErase at any time by answering "N" to the question "Search for more?" when it is displayed.

The capabilities of the NU program are superior to those available in UD. This means that you can use NU to attempt recovery operations which are beyond UD. This is similar to the use of NU after a failure using QU. To delete a directory name, all of the files in that directory must be deleted first. Once the directory name is deleted, QU cannot UnErase those files.

Good housekeeping techniques are also helpful. One is to keep a current listing of the files in your directories. Another is to make regular backup copies of stored data. Making important files "read-only" using the FA program will also reduce the possible accidental erasure of needed files. This will indirectly protect the directory, since it cannot be deleted while it contains active files.

Volume Label

SHORT Directory Name	**VL.COM**
LONG Directory Name	**VOLABEL.COM**
Version 4.0 Directory Name	**VL.EXE**

Until Version 3.0 of DOS, the only way to label a disk volume was during formatting. This meant that renaming required reformatting. VL is a much easier method of accomplishing this task. VL also allows the use of lowercase letters and punctuation. Label length is limited to 11 characters (including spaces)—which happens to be the same as the length of a DOS filename plus extension.

Format: VL [*d:*] [*label-text*] [/L]

The command-line options for VL are:

d: The drive containing the disk to be labeled.

label-text The actual label. Quotes" " must be used to preserve the spaces in a label such as "Disk Two".

/L Used in Version 3.0 and before to allow lowercase letters to be used in the label.

VL can be used to add, change, or delete a disk label without affecting the stored data or directory. VL works either in a semiautomatic or an interactive mode. If the label text is included on the command line. VL writes that label to the disk in the specified drive. Without the label text, VL displays a prompt which includes an 11-space area for the label text to be keyed in.

Using the underscore character "_" as a separator eliminates the need to use quotes when entering *label-text* from the command line. It is not necessary to use quotes when entering the label into the space provided by VL's prompt.

Labels can be very useful to maintain contact with the files stored on that disk. Here's a simple sample:

    A> dir b:

```
Volume in drive B is Working DOS
Directory of B: \
```

Without reading the 30-plus filenames that follow, I know exactly what the files are on this disk.

```
A> dir b:
```

```
Volume in drive B is Letters ARC
Directory of B: \
```

```
84.ARC
85.ARC
86.ARC
```

The disk directory above is of the compressed files of my correspondence. To determine the exact contents of each of those files, another program is required. If I'm only interested in identifying the contents of the disk, this should be enough information.

Listed below are some examples of valid volume names, in both command-line and prompt-line form:

Command Line	Prompt Line
"My Story"	My Story
Part__Three	Part__Three
DirecTIons	DirecTIons
senTInel	senTInel
"backup 1"	backup 1
"CS '86"	CS '86
Rated-XXX	Rated-XXX

Can I use VL on my hard disks?

Yes, the procedure is the same for a hard disk or a diskette.

WipeDisk

Version 3.x Directory Name   **WIPEDISK.COM**
Version 4.0/AE Directory Name   **ïPEDISK.EXE**

WipeDisk overwrites all portions of a disk with a particular binary value. On early versions that value was fixed as a zero (0d, 0h, 00000000b). Starting with Version 3.1, the user is given control of the value to be written, the number of writes, and other parameters.

    The purpose of this is to ensure that a disk can be cleared of any sensitive data before releasing it. It also helps to "wipe" a disk before recycling it. This is especially true if development work is going to be stored on that disk. Sorting through current data and old data at the sector level can be confusing. It can also be frustrating and very time-consuming.

Format: WIPEDISK [*d*:] [*switches*][> | > >]
                 [*device*|*drive/path/filename*]

Here are the command-line options:

d:	The letter of the drive containing the disk to be wiped.
/E	Instructs WipeDisk to overwrite only those areas of the disk which do not contain active files. This is a way to clear "trash" off a disk that is being passed on to another user. It is also a bit of insurance against the problem of cross-linked files when doing a hard disk reorganization. See the questions and answers at the end of this section for an example of how such a problem may be discovered and solved.
/G	Wipes the disk in accordance with the appropriate government specifications.
/LOG	Formats the program output for redirection to either the printer or a disk file.

/Rn	Sets the number of repetitions (times) that the wiping process will be performed. The default is one time. When the /G switch is set, there are three separate wipes, by specification, and this switch is inactive.
/Vn	Sets the value of the character used as the overwrite during the wiping process. The default v. `ue is zero. Any value between 0 and 255 may be specified. This switch may be used with the /G switch.
**>	> >**	The DOS redirection operators. The single ">" redirects the program to a device or file; the double "> >" redirects and appends the program output to an existing filename.

WipeDisk does not have a two-letter abbreviation, which is to prevent using it in error. You must also confirm that you want WipeDisk run by answering "Y" to the prompt, which defaults to No. Pressing the Return key without first pressing the Y key will abort the program without doing anything to the disk. It is also possible to abort WipeDisk while it is running. Pressing the [Ctrl-Break] key combination will stop WipeDisk from proceeding. Data will be lost in those portions of the disk which have been wiped by the process.

WipeDisk begins at the end of the data storage area and works "backward" toward the directory, FAT, and system areas. It is possible to save some information when a disk has been partially wiped. If it runs to completion, WipeDisk overwrites all areas of a disk—system area, FAT, directory, and data storage. Except when the /E switch is used, disks must be reformatted after wiping before they can be reused.

The /G switch writes three different values during three separate passes. On the first pass, all binary ones (15d, 0Fh, 11111111b) are written; on the second, zeros (0d, 0h, 00000000b) are written; and on the third, a value of F6h (246d, 11110110b) is first written and then read. The write/read procedure is done in every sector of the disk. This ensures that all pre-existing data has been removed. The /Vn switch may be used to change the value used in the first two passes; the third value is fixed.

Invoking WipeDisk with the /E switch active overwrites only those areas of the disk which do not currently hold active file, directory, or FAT data. This means that only the information you wish to share is on the disk when you give it to another user. Using SD (Speed Disk) before WipeDisk /E will ensure that there are no fragmented files and no recoverable "extra" data on the unused portion of the disk.

None of the Norton Utilities are copy protected. This means that you can rename any of the programs. Renaming might be another way of preventing problems. Including WipeDisk and WipeFile in batch files with or without renaming the programs is also a possibility. Using a cryptic filename for WipeFile, WipeDisk, and the batch file(s) might provide another level of security from abuse. Putting the /E switch in the batch file with WipeDisk will prevent total data loss on a disk.

The level of protection provided for WipeDisk should equal the protection provided for the FORMAT command. Either has the potential to create a problem. FR (Format Recover) can provide help in the event of an accidental reformat of a hard disk—but there is no recovery from a properly executed WipeDisk.

Is there any way to prevent cross linking?

Yes. Cross linking can only occur when there is data in a cluster that is not overwritten by the new data being placed in that cluster. By using WipeDisk with the /E switch active, all of the inactive space on the disk can be cleared of any remaining data.

Fig. 2-63. Screen report from WipeDisk with the /E switch active. Note the two clusters reported as bad.

```
C:\: c:\util\nu\wipedisk c:/e
WD-Wipe Disk, Advanced Edition, (C) Copr 1987, Peter Norton

Action:        Wipe the Erased data space
Drive:         C:
Wipe count:    1
Wipe value:    0

DANGER! This will wipe-out the erased data space on the entire disk.
Proceed (Y/N) ? [y]

During this operation, you may press
BREAK (Control-C) to interrupt Wipe Disk

Wiping the Erased data space
8,041st cluster: error in writing
8,015th cluster: error in writing
Done

C:\:
```

```
C:\: c:\util\nu\dt /c8041
DT-Disk Test, Advanced Edition, (C) Copr 1987, Peter Norton

Manually marking clusters as Bad
    Cluster 8,041 marked as Bad.


C:\: c:\util\nu\dt /c8015
DT-Disk Test, Advanced Edition, (C) Copr 1987, Peter Norton

Manually marking clusters as Bad
    Cluster 8,015 marked as Bad.
```

I got the display shown in Fig. 2-63 while running WIPEDISK C:/E. What does it mean?

Fig. 2-64. Using Disk Test to mark as bad the two questionable clusters discovered by WipeDisk.

It appears that WipeDisk has had a problem with those two clusters but FORMAT did not. Rather than risk data loss, I would mark those clusters. This means that DOS will recognize them as bad and never again attempt to write data to them. The /C cluster-number switch of the DT utility is designed to do this type of task. As shown in Fig. 2-64 the clusters are marked by number. You can use either DT or WIPEDISK /E to search your disk for bad or questionable clusters.

Fig. 2-65. The Map Disk screen from NU, used here to verify that the two clusters found by WipeDisk are marked as bad. (On the screen, the "B" characters will blink and, on color monitors, be displayed in red.)

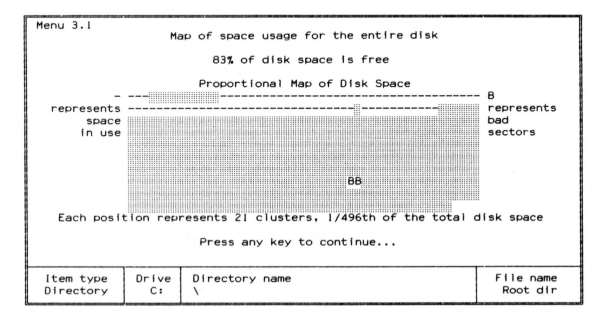

```
 Menu 3.1
                    Map of space usage for the entire disk

                      83% of disk space is free

                    Proportional Map of Disk Space
                 - ---░░░░░░░░---------------------------------- B
  represents    ------------------------------▓----------▓░░░░ represents
       space    ░░░░░░░░░░░░░░░░░░░░░░░░░░░░░░░░░░░░░░░░░░░░░░░ bad
      in use    ░░░░░░░░░░░░░░░░░░░░░░░░░░░░░░░░░░░░░░░░░░░░░░░ sectors
                ░░░░░░░░░░░░░░░░░░░░░░░░░░░░░░░░░░░░░░░░░░░░░░░
                ░░░░░░░░░░░░░░░░░░░░░░░░░░░░░░░░░░░░░░░░░░░░░░░
                ░░░░░░░░░░░░░░░░░░░░░░░░BB░░░░░░░░░░░░░░░░░░░░░
                ░░░░░░░░░░░░░░░░░░░░░░░░░░░░░░░░░░░░░░░░░░░░░░░
                ░░░░░░░░░░░░░░░░░░░░░░░░░░░░░░░░░░░░░░░░░░░░░░
       Each position represents 21 clusters, 1/496th of the total disk space

                     Press any key to continue...


 Item type    Drive    Directory name                       File name
 Directory     C:      \                                    Root dir
```

The screen in Fig. 2-65 is a check to verify that DT did, in fact, mark the clusters as bad. These "B" markings should also be displayed on the disk map that is a part of the SD utility. The only way to remove the B's now is to use DT with the /C cluster-number switch active.

WipeFile

Version 3.x Directory Name   **WIPEFILE.COM**
Version 4.0/AE Directory Name   **WIPEFILE.EXE**

WipeFile is used to overwrite file data areas to prevent anyone from reading what was there. This feature can be used to ensure that data areas are clean before writing new information to the disk, or to prevent out-of-date information from being viewed by others. One file or an entire disk of files may be "wiped." As with WipeDisk, operator confirmation of the parameters is required before WipeFile will run. When more than one filename is specified (i.e., *.COM), WipeFile will also prompt for a yes/no response to confirm the overwriting of each file before actually performing the overwrite.

Format: WIPEFILE [*drive/path*] [*filename*] (space) [*switches*] [>|>>] [*device|drive/path/filename*]

WipeFile offers the following command-line options:

drive/path Tells WipeFile where to find the file to be overwritten. WipeFile must have some type of filename parameter before it will attempt to run.

filename Tells WipeFile which file to overwrite. The DOS global characters * and ? may be used in the filename specification. WipeFile does not have a default mode.

(space) A space is required as a delimiter between the filename and the first switch.

/D An option in Version 3.0 that was later incorporated into WipeFile which deletes the directory listing of the file that has been "wiped."

/G An option (first seen in Version 3.1) that overwrites files to conform to government specifications such as DoD 5220.22-M. When this switch is used, the selected file(s) are wiped a total of three times. The first wipe writes binary 1's, the second writes binary

0's, and the third writes hex value F6. After the last write, WipeFile verifies the write by reading the last value written.

/LOG   Formats the output of WipeFile for redirection to a printer or disk file. First available in Version 3.1.

/N   This is the non-wiping mode. In this mode WipeFile does the same thing as the DOS DELETE command—but WipeFile goes DOS one better by requesting confirmation for each file. When the *.* parameter is used, DOS will ask for only one confirmation before deleting all of the files in the selected directory. WipeFile will require a "yes" response before every file, unless a "no" answer was returned at the "pause/confirm" prompt.

/NOD   In Version 3.1, this option wipes the files but retains the directory listings.

/P   Forces a pause and operator input before acting on each file specified.

/R*n*   Repeats the overwriting procedure *n* times (default is once).

/S   Includes subdirectories in the procedure.

/V*n*   Permits Versions 3.1 and later to accept a decimal value between 0 and 255 as the overwrite value. It will replace the 0 value during a "normal" overwrite and the hex value F6 when the /G switch is toggled on.

Using WipeFile on disks to be recycled can save many headaches. Neither the DOS DELETE nor the FORMAT command removes the information from the file data areas. Until they are overwritten by new information (or by WipeFile or WipeDisk), it is possible to use a program like NU to recover the information.

WipeFile will overwrite hidden, system, or read-only files only when the /P switch is on. This forces the operator to say "yes" when asked if WipeFile is to overwrite this type of file. If the FA (File Attributes) program is used first to remove these attributes, WipeFile will operate normally.

For those who do not "trust" Wipefile to overwrite their data areas adequately, the /R Repetitions switch with its *n* parameter can specify just how many times WipeFile should overwrite the file(s). This is also true of the /V Value switch. Normally, WipeFile uses a binary zero (0) to overwrite, but an operator can specify any decimal value in the range 0 to 255 as the overwrite value.

The /V switch can be used with the /G switch; the /R switch cannot. This is also true of the other mutually exclusive switches. When using the /N No-wipe switch, for example, it would be improper to specify the /Vn or /Rn switches.

Because WipeFile eliminates all possibility of data recovery, it is very unforgiving. It insists on the proper operator input before it

Fig. 2-66. Using WipeFile with A) explicit and B) wild-card file specifications.

A

```
A>wipefile b:arc51.com

WF-Wipe Files, Advanced Edition, (C) Copr 1987, Peter Norton

Action:      Wipe the file
Filename:    ARC51.COM
Wipe count:  1
Wipe value:  0

Directory: B:\
    arc51.com    Wiped clear. Deleted

A>
```

B

```
A>wipefile b:*.*

WF-Wipe Files, Advanced Edition, (C) Copr 1987, Peter Norton

Action:       Wipe the files
Filenames:    *.*
Wipe count:   1
Wipe value:   0

Do you wish confirmation for each file [Y/N] ? N

Directory: B:\
    loader.sys   Read-only file; wiping not allowed.
                 Use /P option or FA program.

    always       Wiped clear. Deleted.
    consult      Wiped clear. Deleted.
    dates        Wiped clear. Deleted.
    for          Wiped clear. Deleted.
    appoint      Wiped clear. Deleted.
    ments        Wiped clear. Deleted.
    gofer        Wiped clear. Deleted.
    broke        Wiped clear. Deleted.
```

attempts to run. This does slow down the process of deleting files. Being forced to consider each file is one way to reduce the number of files that are wiped prematurely.

The first of the two examples shown in Fig. 2-66 uses a full filename, while the second one following uses the asterisk wildcard character. And here is an example of being in a hurry:

A > wipefile b:

WF-Wipe Files, Advanced Edition, (C) Copr 1987, Peter Norton

Must specify files to wipe

A >

The first example in Fig. 2-67 lets you see what WipeFile reports before doing its thing when the /G switch is used. Finally, using a

```
A>wipefile b:*.rbs /g

WF-Wipe Files, Advanced Edition, (C) Copr 1987, Peter Norton

Action:        Wipe the files using government specs.
Filenames:     *.RBS
Wipe count:    1

Wipe File will write 1's, then write 0's, and finally write
the hex value 'F6'. Wipe File will then verify the last
write operation.

Do you wish confirmation for each file [Y/N] ?
```

B

```
A>wipefile b:*.asm /v255/r2

WF-Wipe Files, Advanced Edition, (C) Copr 1987, Peter Norton

Action:        Wipe the files
Filenames:     *.ASM
Wipe count:    2
Wipe value:    255

Do you wish confirmation for each file [Y/N] ? N

Directory: B:\
     1part.asm     Wiped clear 1 times.
    *1part.asm     Wiped clear 2 times. Deleted.
     2part.asm     Wiped clear 1 times.
    *2part.asm     Wiped clear 2 times. Deleted.

A>
```

combination of switches produces a display similar to the second one shown in Fig. 2-67. (Note that the lines marked with asterisks normally overwrite the displayed lines on the screen. If the /LOG switch had been active, only the marked line would have been written.

Read Me

A "Read Me" file is added to the distribution disk(s) when a change has been made which is not reflected in the accompanying documentation. Once you have a hard copy of this file, it need not be copied onto the working copy disk(s). The people at Peter Norton Computing continue to work on the current version while developing new utility programs. The information contained in the READ.ME file will vary over the life of the version.

Format: type [*d:*] read.me [>*device*]

                   print [*d:*] read.me

The command-line options are:

     d: Enter the letter of the drive that contains the Read Me file, if it isn't the default drive.

   >*device*   The name of the device (normally PRN: or LPT1:) where the output is to be sent, instead of to the screen. Use this form if you do not wish to install the DOS print spooler PRINT.

Peter Norton Computing is a responsible and responsive software development company. Their mailing address is clearly printed in the booklet that accompanies the Utilities. If you should find a problem, contact them and get it resolved. It is quite possible that your problem and solution will find its way into a subsequent version of the READ.ME file.

The complete text of the READ.ME file I received with Version 4.0 is shown in Fig. 2-68.

```
Norton Utilities, Version 4.00
Sunday March 1, 1987


Welcome to the Norton Utilities, Version 4.00

To immediately start using the Norton Utilities, just type

    NI

This will start the Norton Integrator, an on-line help program
and "command post" for all of the Norton Utilities.  Now you won't
have to even open the manual!

But you probably will want to since it contains a hands-on tutorial
on UnErasing files, using the main program NU and Quick UnErase.

In addition, we have supplied a small demo program which uses a few
of the features of the Norton Utilities.
```

Fig. 2-68. Text of the READ.ME file from a copy of Version 4.0.

3

NU: The Heart
of the Matter

THIS FIRST PART WILL INTRODUCE THE VARIOUS FEATURES AVAILABLE within the NU program. After the introduction, the more powerful (maybe better described as "dangerous") features will be discussed in more detail. Just remember during this initial tour that the Esc key will back you out of wherever you are and return you to a menu until you reach the main menu. One more press of the Esc key at that point and you will be returned to the DOS prompt.

Like the package itself, the Norton Utility is not "just" a program but a collection of utilities. The opening screen (Fig. 3-1) gives you a preview of what is available.

Notice there are "f" numbers in front of each of the selections. These correspond to the function key which may be pressed to select that feature. The arrow keys (Up and Dn) may also be used to move the reverse video block to the desired location. Version 4.0 and the Advanced Edition change somewhat here (Fig. 3-2). This is due to the new "help" information under the F1 key and the use of the letter keys as "hot" keys.

The window looks familiar, but there have been a few changes. The number of selections has increased, while the amount of information displayed on the screen has decreased. Notice too that the "f" numbers are gone. Now there is an emphasized capital letter in each choice. Pressing that letter key (NU is not case sensitive) will immediately put you into that feature.

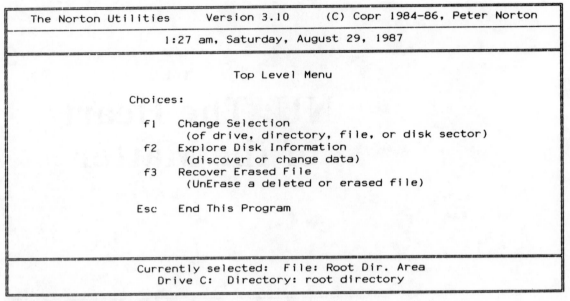

The Norton Utilities   Version 3.10   (C) Copr 1984-86, Peter Norton

1:27 am, Saturday, August 29, 1987

Top Level Menu

Choices:

f1   Change Selection
      (of drive, directory, file, or disk sector)
f2   Explore Disk Information
      (discover or change data)
f3   Recover Erased File
      (UnErase a deleted or erased file)

Esc   End This Program

Currently selected: File: Root Dir. Area
      Drive C: Directory: root directory

Fig. 3-1. The Main menu of NU Version 3.1.

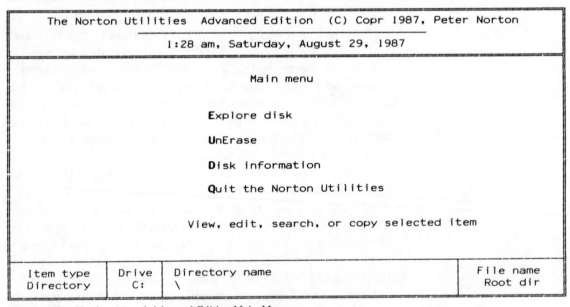

The Norton Utilities Advanced Edition (C) Copr 1987, Peter Norton

1:28 am, Saturday, August 29, 1987

Main menu

Explore disk

UnErase

Disk information

Quit the Norton Utilities

View, edit, search, or copy selected item

Item type	Drive	Directory name	File name
Directory	C:	\	Root dir

Fig. 3-2. The Version 4.0 and Advanced Edition Main Menu.

The information at the bottom of the window is the same. It has been reorganized to make it easier to read. Note too that the comment about the Esc key is missing. Never fear—it still works fine. The short phrases, enclosed in parentheses, that were on the screen before are now displayed only when the reverse video block is over that selection.

Learning About Your Disks

The explanation is for the Explore Disk selection. What you can discover about your hard or floppy disk with this selection will depend on how long you want to wander through the menus and look at the information that NU can display at your request. The screen representation shown in Fig. 3-3 is an example of the technical information available about a standard floppy disk. Similar information is available about other types of floppy disks and also hard disks.

Mapping the space usage of a disk can reveal fragmentation. The Version 4.0 screen represented in Fig. 3-4 indicates there are unused clusters within the files stored on this floppy disk.

The screen shown in Fig. 3-5 indicates the cluster(s) which hold a specific file (in this case LOADER.SYS). If the SD (Speed Disk) program were to look at this disk, it would display this file as one that must have a fixed position (indicated by the use of the capital "X") on the disk. It would also eliminate those unused clusters by moving some of the other files around. This increases the speed with which data can be transferred from the disk to the system RAM.

If you want further information about a specific item, you will first have to tell NU which item. There are a few differences between the versions at this point also. Making a selection when using Version 3.X required either pressing a function key or using the cursor control keys to move the reverse video over the desired choice; then the Return key is pressed.

Fig. 3-3. Specifications for a double-sided diskette produced by the Technical Information option of Version 4.0/Advanced Edition.

```
Menu 3.2
                         Technical information

          Drive A:

          Type of disk:
             Double-sided, double-density, 8-sector

          Basic storage capacity:
             320 thousand characters (kilobytes)
             37% of disk space is free

          Logical dimensions:
             Sectors are made up of 512 bytes
             Tracks are made up of 8 sectors per disk side
             There are 2 disk sides
             The disk is made up of 40 tracks
             Space for files is allocated in clusters of 2 sectors
             There are 315 clusters
             Each cluster is 1,024 bytes
             The disk's root directory can hold 112 files

                    Press any key to continue...
```

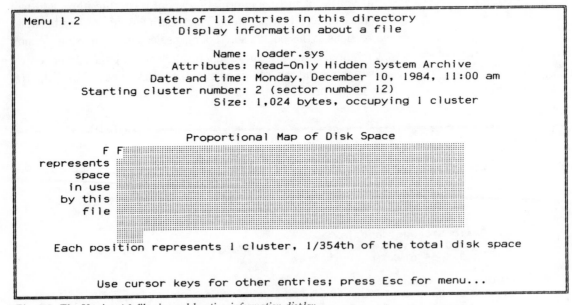

```
Menu 3.1              Map of space usage for the entire disk

                       85% of disk space is free

                     Proportional Map of Disk Space

            _   ::::::::: --- ::::::::::::::: --------------------------
represents  ----------------------------:::::
    space            ::::::::::::::::::::::::::::::::::::::::::::::::
   in use           ::::::::::::::::::::::::::::::::::::::::::::::::
                    ::::::::::::::::::::::::::::::::::::::::::::::::
                    ::::::::::::::::::::::::::::::::::::::::::::::::
                    ::::::::::::::::::::::::::::::::::::::::::::::::

        Each position represents 1 cluster, 1/354th of the total disk space

                     Press any key to continue...


  Item type    Drive   Directory name                    File name
  Directory    A:      \                                 Root dir
```

Fig. 3-4. Space utilization map produced by Version 4.0.

```
Menu 1.2              16th of 112 entries in this directory
                      Display information about a file

                        Name: loader.sys
                  Attributes: Read-Only Hidden System Archive
               Date and time: Monday, December 10, 1984, 11:00 am
      Starting cluster number: 2 (sector number 12)
                        Size: 1,024 bytes, occupying 1 cluster


                     Proportional Map of Disk Space

            F F::::::::::::::::::::::::::::::::::::::::::::::::
represents    ::::::::::::::::::::::::::::::::::::::::::::::::
    space     ::::::::::::::::::::::::::::::::::::::::::::::::
   in use     ::::::::::::::::::::::::::::::::::::::::::::::::
  by this     ::::::::::::::::::::::::::::::::::::::::::::::::
     file     ::::::::::::::::::::::::::::::::::::::::::::::::
              ::::::::::::::::::::::::::::::::::::::::::::::::

        Each position represents 1 cluster, 1/354th of the total disk space

             Use cursor keys for other entries; press Esc for menu...
```

Fig. 3-5. The Version 4.0 file size and location information display.

The first Change Selection screen, shown in Fig. 3-6 comes from Version 3.1. In Version 4.0 and the Advanced Edition (Fig. 3-7), the function keys are not used. Pressing the key corresponding to the emphasized capital letter in the selection desired will move you immediately to that feature. The expansion of the selection meaning is again displayed

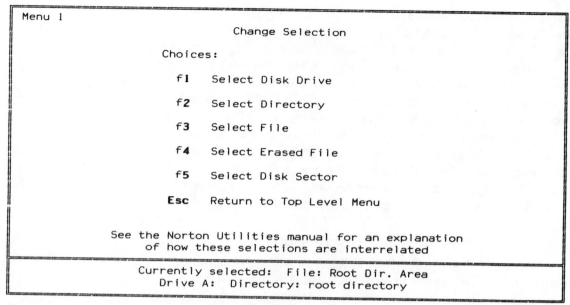

```
Menu 1
                      Change Selection
               Choices:

                  f1    Select Disk Drive

                  f2    Select Directory

                  f3    Select File

                  f4    Select Erased File

                  f5    Select Disk Sector

                  Esc   Return to Top Level Menu


         See the Norton Utilities manual for an explanation
            of how these selections are interrelated

         Currently selected:  File: Root Dir. Area
            Drive A:  Directory: root directory
```

Fig. 3-6. The Change Selection menu from Version 3.1 of NU.

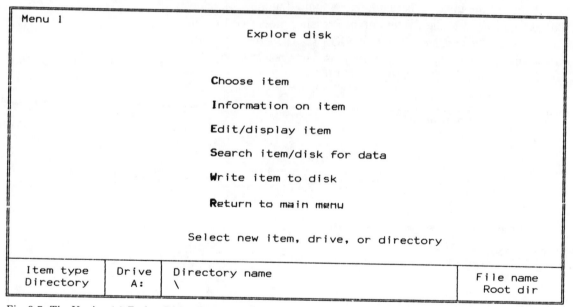

```
Menu 1
                       Explore disk


                  Choose item

                  Information on item

                  Edit/display item

                  Search item/disk for data

                  Write item to disk

                  Return to main menu

              Select new item, drive, or directory

  Item type    Drive    Directory name            File name
  Directory    A:       \                          Root dir
```

Fig. 3-7. The Version 4.0 Explore Disk selection menu.

below the selection list. It changes to match the location of the reverse video block.

The information displayed by the window for selecting a specific file or subdirectory when using version 4.0 or the AE is much more detailed. Notice that there are reverse video blocks across the bottom of the screen. These indicate the active Function Keys. *Do not press the F6 function key!* This takes you into the partition table of your hard disk (Fig. 3-8). Less than skillful modification of the information stored there can ruin a hard disk. (We will get into more detail about the partition table a bit later in this chapter.) I find the F9 key very comforting: It is the "UnDo" key, and it does what it says. All modifications made before pressing the Return key are canceled.

Using the cursor control keys are the only way to select the file to be investigated in the older versions. Starting with Version 4.0/Advanced Edition, the "Speed Search" capability has been added. This means that by pressing the Tab key and then pressing the first letter or two of the filename will move the reverse video block to that file (Fig. 3-9).

A Brief Anatomy Lesson

Before going too much further, let's look at what some of these entries are. The beginning of a hard disk is called the *partition table*. This is the one place that inexperienced users should avoid.

The display shown in Fig. 3-10 indicates that nothing has been done to any of the tables. There are only a limited number of values that can be placed in the System area. Pressing the space bar will cycle through those values. They are DOS-12, DOS-16, and ?—the question mark indicating that the partition is used by a non-DOS operating system, such as XENIX, DX10, or PC/PICK.

Fig. 3-8. The boot area of a disk, shown in Text format.

```
┌ Boot area ═══════════════════════════════════ Text format ═┐
│ Sector 0 in Boot area                        Offset 0, hex 00
│
│   .4.IBM   3.3........)......3....¦...x6.7.V.S?+¦...&.=t.&..........G...+¦..
│   .rg .¦..&.¦...¦...¦.?¦.7¦.  .&.¦..¦..Hw...7¦...?¦.......r......}..u
│
│   . ..}...t..w}.j2...^....D.....}.....3..6¦...<¦.7¦.=¦...7¦.I..¦*.;¦@8.<¦s.
│   .<¦PhNXrF (.<¦t..7¦.&¦.......¦...}..=¦.p..t".........3..6.¦....;¦3..6<end-f
│   ile-marker>¦..*¦.9¦.....9¦....6;¦........}.6*¦...
│   Non-System disk or disk error
│   Replace and strike any key when ready
│
│   Disk Boot failure
│   IBMBIO  COMIBMDOS   COM.U*
│
│
│
│
│
│
│
│                      Press Enter to continue
│ ╵Help    2Hex     3Text    4Dir    5FAT    6Partn  7        8        9Undo    10QuitNU
```

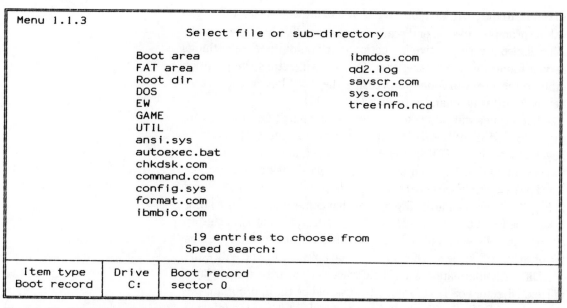

```
Menu 1.1.3
                         Select file or sub-directory

                   Boot area                ibmdos.com
                   FAT area                 qd2.log
                   Root dir                 savscr.com
                   DOS                      sys.com
                   EW                       treeinfo.ncd
                   GAME
                   UTIL
                   ansi.sys
                   autoexec.bat
                   chkdsk.com
                   command.com
                   config.sys
                   format.com
                   ibmbio.com


                     19 entries to choose from
                   Speed search:

  Item type      Drive   Boot record
  Boot record     C:     sector 0
```

Fig. 3-9. The Select File or Sub-Directory menu from the Advanced Edition.

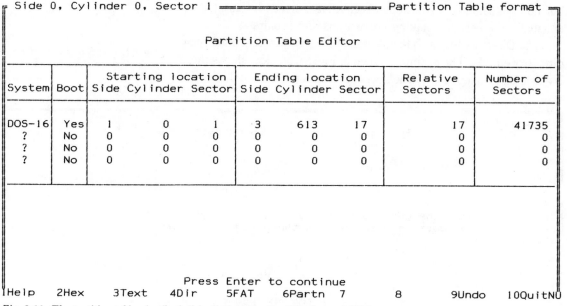

System	Boot	Starting location Side Cylinder Sector			Ending location Side Cylinder Sector			Relative Sectors	Number of Sectors
DOS-16	Yes	1	0	1	3	613	17	17	41735
?	No	0	0	0	0	0	0	0	0
?	No	0	0	0	0	0	0	0	0
?	No	0	0	0	0	0	0	0	0

Side 0, Cylinder 0, Sector 1 ============================ Partition Table format

Partition Table Editor

Press Enter to continue

```
1Help    2Hex    3Text   4Dir    5FAT    6Partn  7      8      9Undo   10QuitNU
```

Fig. 3-10. The partition table of a fixed disk, displayed by the NU advanced Edition.

In the "Boot" area there are only two possibilities, Yes or No. Only one partition at a time can have a Yes answer, meaning that's the system to be loaded on power-up; the space bar will cycle these choices.

If editing in Hex is easier, press the F2 key and then the F6 key to return to the partition table. When you exit the partition table, you will be prompted to save or discard any changes that have been made. This is also a very positive indication that you did not leave things as you found them. Pressing the "D" key will return the partition table to the way you found it; pressing the "W" key or the Return key will write the changes to disk (Fig. 3-11).

The proper way to make changes to the partition table is with the DOS FDISK utility. It is possible to modify the partition table beyond the ability of FDISK to repair, however, and it is also possible to prevent FORMAT from accessing the hard disk again.

The first visible area on the listing of files and subdirectories shown in Fig. 3-9 is the Boot area. Right after that comes the FAT area (Fig. 3-12). The FAT, or *File Allocation Table*, is the record of what clusters are occupied by which files. The root directory shows the first cluster of the file. This is all DOS needs to be able to find the entire file.

Different information is available when certain areas are displayed in Hex, Directory or Text format. Text would be the appropriate way to view an ASCII file. The root directory in Text is not too informative (Fig. 3-13). The Hex format (Fig. 3-14) provides more information, but how valuable it is will depend on what is needed. This format is usually the best for making corrections and repairs.

The Directory format is the most useful for viewing and modifying directory entries. The example shown in Fig. 3-15 below shows there is a deleted filename and a disk label in this directory. All of the entries

Fig. 3-11. The Save or Discard menu from Version 4.0 and the Advanced Edition.

```
Menu 1.3
                    Save or discard changes made to data



         You have made changes to the cluster in memory

         (Changes are made and shown highlighted when
          data is displayed in the hexadecimal format)



              Write the changed data

              Review the changed data

              Discard the changes


          Write the changes to disk
```

```
    3         4      5      6      7      8      9     10     11    12 <EOF>    14
      15     16     17     18     19     20     21     22     23    24    25    26
      27 <EOF> <EOF> <EOF> <EOF> <EOF> <EOF> <EOF> <EOF> <EOF> <EOF> <EOF>
  <EOF>     40     41     42     43     44     45     46     47    48    49    50
      51 <EOF>     53 <EOF> <EOF>     56     57     58     59    60 <EOF>    62
      63     64     65 <EOF> <EOF>     68     69 <EOF> <EOF> <EOF> <EOF>    74
      75 <EOF>     77     78     79     80     81     82     83    84    85    86
      87     88     89 <EOF>     91     92     93     94     95    96    97    98
  <EOF>    100    101    102 <EOF>    104    105    106 <EOF>   108   109   110
     111    112    113    114 <EOF>    116    117    118    119   120   121 <EOF>
     123    124    125    126 <EOF>    128    129    130    131 <EOF>   133   134
     135    136    137 <EOF>    139    140    141    142    143   144   145   146
     147 <EOF>    149    150    151    152    153    154    155   156   157   158
     159    160    161    162    163    164    165    166 <EOF>   168   169   170
     171    172    173    174    175    176    177    178    179   180   181   182
     183    184    185    186    187    188    189    190    191   192   193   194
     195    196    197    198    199    200    201    202    203   204   205   206
     207    208    209    210    211    212    213    214    215   216   217   218
     219    220    221    222    223    224    225    226    227   228   229   230
```

Press Enter to continue

1Help   2Hex   3Text   4Dir   5FAT   6Partn 7   8   9Undo   10QuitNU

Fig. 3-12. The File Allocation Table (FAT) area, as displayed by the Advanced Edition.

```
IBMBIO  COM''r..TVIBMDOS  COM''q.
.uUTIL      .Awv..DOS          .m...EW         ..!.GAME          .!.CONFIG  S
YS ..!&2COMMAND COM `q.'.bQD2      LOG 8..4.AUTOEXECBAT J!6@FORMAT  COM `r
.7`-CHKDSK  COM `r.=z&ANSI    SYS `q.B..SYS      COM `q.C..TREEINFONCD F..
F.SAVSCR  COM R;G..
```

Press Enter to continue

1Help   2Hex   3Text   4Dir   5FAT   6Partn 7   8   9Undo   10QuitNU

Fig. 3-13. The root directory in Text format (Version 4.0).

in the root directory may be changed. NU will limit the modifications to valid values. This does not mean that access is protected. It means that 13/32/99 is not a valid date and will not be allowed. Time has similar limitations. Any DOS valid hour is accepted.

145

```
┌ Root dir ═══════════════════════════════════════════════ Hex format ═
│ Sector 83 in root directory                              Offset 0, hex 00
│49424D42 494F2020 434F4D27 00000000 00000000 00000060 IBMBIO   COM'..........`
│720E0200 54560000 49424D44 4F532020 434F4D27 00000000 r▲●.TV..IBMDOS   COM'....
│00000000 00000060 710E0D00 CF750000 5554494C 20202020 .......`q▲......UTIL....
│20202010 00000000 00000000 00004177 F60E1C00 00000000 ▶.........Aw÷▲─......
│444F5320 20202020 20202020 00000000 00000000 00006D88 DOS        ▶..........mê
│F60E1D00 00000000 45572020 20202020 20202010 00000000 ÷▲↔......EW        ▶....
│00000000 0000C800 21001E00 00000000 47414D45 20202020 ......╚.!.▲.....GAME
│20202010 00000000 00000000 00000B0B 21001F00 00000000 ▶...........!.▼..
│434F4E46 49472020 53595320 00000000 00000000 00008F0E CONFIG   SYS ..........À▲
│21002600 32000000 434F4D4D 414E4420 434F4D20 00000000 !.&.2...COMMAND COM .....
│00000000 00000060 710E2700 DB620000 51443220 20202020 .......`q▲'.■b..QD2
│4C4F4720 00000000 00000000 00003800 060F3400 860C0000 LOG ..........8.♠.4.å▼..
│4155544F 45584543 42415420 00000000 00000000 00004A00 AUTOEXECBAT ..........J.
│21003600 40000000 464F524D 41542020 434F4D20 00000000 !.6.@...FORMAT  COM .....
│00000000 00000060 720E3700 602D0000 43484B44 534B2020 .......`r▲7.`-..CHKDSK
│434F4D20 00000000 00000000 00000060 720E3D00 7A260000 COM ..........`r▲=.z&..
│414E5349 20202020 53595320 00000000 00000000 00000060 ANSI     SYS ..........`
│710E4200 8E060000 53595320 20202020 434F4D20 00000000 q▲B.Ä▲..SYS     COM .....
│00000000 00000060 710E4300 9E120000 54524545 494E464F .......`q▲C.₨‡..TREEINFO
│4E434420 00000000 00000000 0000468B 010F4600 BB000000 NCD ..........Fï☺.F.╗...
│53415653 43522020 434F4D20 00000000 00000000 00000052 SAVSCR   COM ..........R
│3B0B4700 AD060000          Press Enter to continue     ;.G.¡♠..
│1Help    2Hex    3Text   4Dir    5FAT     6Partn  7       8         9Undo   10QuitNU
```

Fig. 3-14. The root directory in Hex format (Version 4.0).

```
┌ Root dir ═══════════════════════════════════════════ Directory format ═
│ Sector 83 in root directory                          Offset 0, hex 00
│                                                          Attributes
│Filename Ext     Size     Date      Time     Cluster  Arc R/O Sys Hid Dir Vol
│─────────.───────═══════  ════════  ════════ ═══════  ═══════════════════════
│IBMBIO   COM     22100    3/18/87   12:00 pm      2   Arc R/O Sys Hid
│IBMDOS   COM     30159    3/17/87   12:00 pm     13   Arc R/O Sys Hid
│UTIL                      7/22/87    2:58 pm     28                   Dir
│DOS                       7/22/87    5:03 pm     29                   Dir
│EW                        1/01/80   12:06 am     30                   Dir
│GAME                      1/01/80    1:24 am     31                   Dir
│CONFIG   SYS        50    1/01/80    1:52 am     38   Arc
│COMMAND  COM     25307    3/17/87   12:00 pm     39   Arc
│QD2      LOG      3206    8/06/87   12:01 am     52   Arc
│AUTOEXEC BAT        64    1/01/80   12:02 am     54   Arc
│FORMAT   COM     11616    3/18/87   12:00 pm     55   Arc
│CHKDSK   COM      9850    3/18/87   12:00 pm     61   Arc
│ANSI     SYS      1678    3/17/87   12:00 pm     66   Arc
│SYS      COM      4766    3/17/87   12:00 pm     67   Arc
│TREEINFO NCD       187    8/01/87    5:26 pm     70   Arc
│SAVSCR   COM      1709    9/27/85   10:16 am     71   Arc
│═════════.═══════ ═══════ ════════  ════════ ═══════  ═══════════════════════
│                          Press Enter to continue
│1Help    2Hex    3Text   4Dir    5FAT     6Partn  7       8         9Undo   10QuitNU
```

Fig. 3-15. The root directory in Directory format (Version 4.0).

Why can't I use the "Speed Search" to get to the Boot, Fat, or root directory areas?

In the file mode NU reads the files just like DOS does. These are not true DOS files.

146

Why is there a "Create a file" selection available when trying to UnErase a file?

When a file has lost its filename from the directory, a new filename must be created so that the remaining sectors can be collected and linked.

Can .EXE and .COM files be recovered in the same way text files are?

Yes, and it's just as easy, so long as you can read the code as easily as you can read text.

Solutions to Common Problems

Just how much or how little can be recovered or changed using one of the Norton Utilities?

FR (Format Recover) may be able to recover all 32 megabytes of a hard disk that has been reformatted. UD (Unremove Directory) may be able to recover the directory name and all of the files that were in it. QU (Quick UnErase) may be able to recover a file that has been deleted. NU (Norton Utility) may be able to recover file fragments.

I need to recover a large group of files. What is the best way to do it? None of them have been overwritten.

Using the UnErase routine within the NU program, begin with the smallest files and try to recover them one at a time. If problems occur, delete the corrupted file and try recovering a different file. Patience is mandatory in this type of a recovery operation. Also, deleting recovered files several more times as you work through, trying to recover all of the data, is harmless.

After reformatting my hard disk, I can't get it to boot the system.

Two hidden files and the COMMAND.COM file must be on any disk before it is "bootable." IBMBIO.COM (or IO.SYS) and IBMDOS.COM (or MSDOS.SYS) are the hidden files that are copied from your DOS system disk to another disk by the SYS *d*: command, where *d*: is the drive designator of the disk location. Using the COPY command will transfer the COMMAND.COM file to the new disk. Since the hidden files must be in a specific place on the new disk, using the COPY command will not transfer them properly. Also, COPY cannot transfer files whose Hidden attribute bit is set.

My list of directories and subdirectories is so long that it runs off the screen.

The DOS DIR command with either the /P (pause) or /W (wide) switch is one way to do it. The LD (List Directories) utility with the /W (wide) and /A (all) switches will provide a wide format, five filenames/directorynames on each line without the size and date stamp, listing of all the files in all of the drives. The output of these commands can be directed to the printer so that a permanent copy is available for reference. The DOS TREE command also will provide this information in a different format. Using the printer toggle will make a hard copy.

I can't remember where all of my files are stored. Also, I'm not sure if I have duplicate copies in different directories and subdirectories.

The FF (File Find) utility can be used to search one disk/drive or all drives to find files by name, extension, or partial name. If the global default *.* is used, then all of the files will be listed. The listing may be redirected to the printer or by toggling the printer to print the display, you can read the filenames while a hard copy is being made.

My disks are getting full. I need some way to make sure there is no wasted space, and also a means to offload some of the files to floppy disks. I don't want to lose any files because of lack of space on the floppy.

SD (Speed Disk) will reorganize the directories and files so that the "slack" or "wasted" space is as small as possible. Then use this form of FS:

FS *filespec d*:

where *d*: is the target disk will verify there is adequate space on the disk for the files(s).

I know the text. I just can't remember the name of the file where I wrote it.

TS (Text Search) specifying the text string and using the DOS wildcard characters probably can find it. TS is not case-sensitive, so it is not necessary to retain the same capitalization. It is context-sensitive, however, so the wording must match.

How can I be sure that a diskette I want to fill with important information is good?

DT (Disk Test) will test the entire disk and provide you with a report, on screen or printer, of the disk condition.

I've used the DOS SORT command and it helped. What I really need is a way to sort files according to my needs.

DS (Directory Sort) can automatically sort the way the DOS utility does, or it can be used interactively to give you total control over the listing order of the files.

How can I be sure that the disks I send out contain only the data I want sent?

WIPEDISK writes a value, or sequence of values, to every sector of the disk. Using the /G switch will also have WIPEDISK read each sector to ensure that only the latest value is recorded there.

I just want to be very sure that a file I just deleted cannot be recovered and read.

WIPEFILE does the same type of total erasing as WIPEDISK on a file-by-file basis. It even removes the deleted filename from the directory. After this type of removal, neither QU or NU can recover the file and none of the utilities will list the filename in a directory listing.

I'm trying to help a friend with a problem and he doesn't know much about his computer. How can I get the information without taking his system apart?

SI (System Information) can provide most of the specific information you might need.

Is there an easy way to print out text or source code files, with line numbers?

LP (Line Print) can provide a means of printing text files and including line numbers. The DOS PRINT or TYPE commands also can be used if the other formatting options of LP are not desired. Neither of the DOS options will provide line numbers unless they are present in the source code file. (Using the DOS "pipe" redirector with the FIND filter can generate line-numbered output, considerably less elegantly than LP.)

I want to put volume labels on my disks without reformatting them. They are currently formatted and filled using DOS 2.0.

VL (Volume Label) will write volume labels on formatted disks, full or empty. VL will also let you change or delete an existing volume label.

How can I keep track of the time I use my computer? Is there any way to time various operations performed by my computer?

TM (Time Mark) can be included in batch files to automatically figure the length of time taken by various tasks. This is a redirectable routine that can be retained as a printed or disk record.

Is there any way to change the default colors on my color monitor?

Using SA (Screen Attributes) in various ways can make computer displays more colorful and, through selection of appropriate colors, very meaningful.

Is there any way to have the computer tell me when it has finished a task?

SA (Screen Attributes) and BEEP can be used to provide visual and audible indications of a task termination.

I've heard that disk "crashes" can be expensive. Can you explain this?

Losing data from a disk can be a serious problem if there is no other copy of it. Loss of access to the information stored on a disk may be even more serious. To keep the time, information, and monetary loss to a minimum, regular disk and file maintenance must be an important part of operating the computer.

One way to make sure that the least possible amount of data is lost is to back up all of the files that have had changes made to them during that session. DOS will activate the Archive attribute automatically. By running FR (Format Recover) at the end of each session, the loss can also be reduced.

Careful storage of disks and tapes is also very important. This includes the careful use of working copies of disks. Try not to leave disks exposed to the environment. When not in use, the disks should be in their envelopes and in a storage case. Unless required by copy protection, do not use the original disks that came with the software package; make and use a copy.

When programs on a hard disk are changed, be sure to update the backup copy.

I have a Bernoulli Box. Will I have trouble using the Norton Utilities?

The Norton Utilities from Version 3.1 upward are fully compatible with the Bernoulli Box.

Will I have any problems installing the Norton Utilities in my system?

The Norton Utilities are not copy protected and should not cause any problems being installed or copied on any type of mass storage device.

I want to be able to use the Norton Utilities on my portable computer.

You may copy the programs from the 5.25-inch disk onto any other type of MS-DOS disk, 3.5-inch or 1.2 megabyte. At present, the Utilities are distributed only on the 360K, 5.25-inch diskette.

Is it necessary for me to have a color monitor to use the Norton Utilities?

No, color is not necessary. In fact, some of the programs do not support color and may switch your monitor to the black-and-white mode. Upon exiting that program, your monitor's color mode is not restored. Issuing the command:

MODE CO80 (that's "cee-oh-eight-zero")

will restore your monitor to the color mode and 80 columns of text.

I've used the /LOG switch but nothing goes to the printer.

The /LOG switch only prepares the program output for printing or writing to disk; there are no overwrites of messages you see on the screen. To print the information, you must use the DOS redirect ">" or redirect-and-append ">>" operator together with a device (LPTI or PRN) or filename (if you want the information written to a disk file). Examples of the DOS operator use are:

TM start /log>LPTI

This will send the information to the printer.

TM start /log>>A:tasks.

This will add or append the information to the end of the file in the A: drive named TASKS. If this file does not exist, DOS will create the file and then write the information to it.

I deleted a file and am continuing to use the disk. Can I still recover the information in that file?

If the data area containing the information has not been overwritten with new information, you should be able to recover it. Full recovery is by no means a sure thing, however, and your chances decrease with every disk access. This is why, when you inadvertently delete a file, you should *immediately* reach for NU of QU.

I cannot find the filename of a deleted file in the directory.

DOS has reused the directory space. This does not mean that it has used all of the file space. Partial recovery of the information may still be possible.

Why is there a Disk Test (DT) program in the Utilities when DOS includes a CHKDSK utility?

CHKDSK checks for the logical errors; DT checks for physical errors. Also, it is possible to mark bad sectors using DT, without having to reformat the disk.

FA (File Attributes) allows me to hide filenames, is there any reason I might want to do this?

One reason you might consider hiding some files is that they are only called by a batch file. Hiding them will remove them from the listing displayed by the DIR command.

The DOS REName command allows me to rename files. How can I rename directories?

Using only DOS commands requires that you make the new directory (MD), copy the files from the old directory to the new one, delete all the files in the old directory, and finally remove (with RMDIR) the old directory itself. Using the NU (Norton Utility) program, you can change the name while leaving the files in place. It's a much faster and simpler solution, which also retains the integrity of the files. If fragmentation is suspected, use the SD (Speed Disk) program to eliminate the problem.

Is it possible to eliminate the C> prompt from my display completely?

With careful programming, error-free data entry and enough effort, it is possible. A better question would be, "Is it practical to eliminate the C> prompt from my display?" The answer to this question is "yes" if the desired number of applications is fixed. In many cases, "no" would be the more correct answer.

Programming around the DOS prompt will requires disk space, and it will take time to run these new programs before reaching the desired application. Moreover, writing closed-loop ASK menus, so that you always return to a menu screen after running your application, can limit your direct access to DOS commands on those occasions when you really need them. Fortunately, there is a slick but little-used way to provide DOS access without having to abort your menu batch file, so you can offer both "Quit" and "Use DOS" options.

DOS allows you to run multiple copies of the COMMAND.COM program, a technique known in PC jargon as "loading a secondary command processor." Simply type COMMAND at the DOS prompt.

You'll get another prompt (following a DOS version message), you'll be able to perform DOS operations—even run programs—and whatever you had been doing will be put on hold. Type EXIT at the (secondary) DOS prompt and you'll return to the process that had been running when you invoked a second copy of COMMAND.COM. To prove this to yourself, try the simple batch file COMTEST.BAT.

```
copy con: comtest.bat
echo off
echo Loading secondary command processor . . .
prompt [$P]    rem leave a space after right bracket
COMMAND
echo Secondary processor terminated
prompt      rem make this your normal prompt
echo on
^Z
```

When the bracketed prompt comes up, do a few DIRs and other DOS operations; then type EXIT and press Return.

Why have LD (List Directories) and NCD (Norton Change Directories)?

LD (List Directories) is not an interactive program. It provides only a text or tree (graphic) listing of the directories on the specified drive. NCD (Norton Change Directories) is an interactive program which permits the creation of new directories (MD command) or the deletion (RD command) of existing empty directories. Additionally it permits direct changes (CD command) from one directory to another without having to enter the entire pathname.

Two methods of moving from directory to directory are available from within NCD. When the directory name is known, enter NCD *directoryname* at the C> prompt and press Return. When you don't remember the directory name, simply enter NCD. This will take you to the interactive graphic mode of NCD. Then, using the cursor control keys, you can search the entire tree structure for the desired directory. With the reverse video over the directory name, pressing Return will move you immediately to that directory. NCD provides all of the needed intermediate directory names to build the full DOS-required pathname.

It's all very nice that a user with a hard disk can have all these nice menus, etc., but I only have two diskette drives.

```
IO.SYS                 ; (hidden) req'd by system
MSDOS.SYS              ; (hidden) req'd by system
COMMAND.COM            ; bootable disk
CLOCK.COM              ; set system time
WP.COM                 ; printer spooler program
UNDERSB.COM            ; change the cursor
PKLOAD.COM             ; ProKey
TIPCBUFF.COM           ; expand keyboard buffer to 147
                       ; keystrokes
PROKEY.COM             ; ProKey
AUTOEXEC.BAT           ; see A.BAT
CRSR.COM               ; cursor change program
CCLOCK.COM             ; digital clock in top rh. corner
A.BAT                  ; contains
   CLOCK/S             ; set system time
   EMULATE             ; emulate an IBM compatible
   WP/M=128            ; 128K spooler
   TIPCBUFF            ; buffer
   CRSR 2              ; underscore slow blink
   CCLOCK              ; digital clock
```

Fig. 4-1. Sample of a startup disk that can be used for word processing.

Is there any way that I can do at least some of these neat things?

Using a startup disk, you can customize the configuration of the system using the CONFIG.SYS file. To gain the maximum efficiency and flexibility from this technique, the startup disks should be designed for specific uses. Fig. 4-1 shows an example of a startup disk for word processing.

When the A> prompt returns, remove the startup disk from Drive A and insert the word processor system disk. Drive B is used for the disk containing the text files. I keep different types of correspondence on different disks. This scheme permits changing "folders" without leaving the word processor. It's not as efficient or as quick as having a hard disk, but there are a few pluses. Disk capacity limits the individual folder size, but an unlimited number of disks provide unlimited total capacity. Removable floppy disks can be easily secured or transported.

If a CONFIG.SYS file with the line:

DEVICE = ANSI.SYS

is also on the startup disk along with the SA utility, then a line like:

SA BRIGHT YELLOW on BLUE

can be included in an AUTOEXEC.BAT file. Depending on your word processor, this could be a comfortable combination for writing letters.

The idea of using customized startup disks is neat. Can something similar be done on a system that is set up to boot from the hard disk?

Yes, if there is a bootable disk in Drive A, the system will boot from Drive A and not the hard disk. This will permit customizing via the CONFIG.SYS file. Then a simple C:\ASK main as the last or only line in an AUTOEXEC.BAT file will display the main menu you have designed. It might be just as easy to go directly to the application program. This would save some time because it bypasses the ASK menu programs completely.

I have already written some customizing .BAT files in the various directories of my hard disk. Will these have to be removed or changed now that I'm going to be using ASK to integrate everything?

No, the action code line(s) within the ASK program can call the .BAT file as easily as it can any other program. Or, the last line of the .BAT file on the startup disk can call the .BAT file in the hard disk application program directory.

What do I do when I finish using the word processor and want to use something like R:base 5000?

It could be as simple as 1, 2, 3.

1. Remove the text files disk from Drive A.
2. Insert the R:base startup disk.
3. Warm-boot the system. (Press the Ctrl, Alt, and Del keys all at the same time.)

This will allow you to use the CONFIG.SYS file with a different number of files and/or buffers, along with the DEVICE = ANSI.SYS line. Depending on your preference, the AUTOEXEC.BAT file can then take you to the R:base menu or an ASK menu.

Afterword

A SIGNIFICANT PORTION OF MY WORK WITH NEW USERS INVOLVES teaching them how to do things right the first time. The balance of that training is teaching them how to recover from the mistakes they make or the accidents that do happen.

Murphy's first law states, "If anything can go wrong, it will, and at the worst possible moment." Over the years I have seen this proved repeatedly. Since I have been unable to devise any way to keep myself from making errors—short of doing nothing, which is a mistake—and I cannot control accidents, I have learned how to fix things. This "fixing" ability is not universal. I have been responsible for many things that I have not been able to fix. In some cases there is an alternative, and in others there isn't. Where no alternative is available, only an apology and corrective action are expected.

I have a closet full of tools and parts that I use to keep various things in working order or to repair broken ones. The Norton Utilities are a closet full of tools for software repairs. They are also useful for preventing breakdowns. Learn how to use them before the need arises.

Learning how to use the NU program alone will take time and concentration. Invest the time and effort before irreplaceable data must be recovered. Knowing exactly how to recover data will insure that none of the recoverable data is permanently lost.

Every situation is not covered and every question has not been answered. When you discover something useful, let one of us know.

Peter Norton's address and phone number are in the user manual you received with the Norton Utilities. I can be reached on DELPHI as username ELLISCO via mail at any time and on-line most evenings after 9 P.M. Eastern time. Sharing your experience with others will help them by making all of us aware of some of the potential problems that can occur and how they can be corrected. It can also help Peter Norton Computing by making them aware of the needs of the users of their software. Nothing is perfect. In spite of this, many of us are working at ways to make this lack of perfection a bit easier to cope with. Your assistance is therefore necessary and much appreciated. And, just in case one of us forgets to say it later, Thank you very much for sharing your knowledge, problems and solutions with us and everyone else.

Index

REPORT option, 108
RN, 30
root directory, 145-146

S

SA.COM, 99
SA.EXE, 99
Save or Discard menu, 29, 144
SCRATR.COM, 99
Screen Attribute (SA), 10, 99-107, 152
  hardware requirements for, 100
screen attributes program, 2
screen color, 19, 99, 152
  setting of, 10, 88
  using COLORS.BAT to evaluate,
    100-106
SD.EXE, 108
search routine, 118
Select File menu, 25, 42, 143
setup files, 77
SHORT.BAT, 12
SI.COM, 112
SI.EXE, 112
signature files, 11
  finding, 52
  use of Directory Sort (DS), 35
slack space, 64
  reduction of, 90, 150
sort keys, values for, 33
sorting directories and subdirectories,
  33
source code files, printing of, 152
space requirements, 7
space utilization map, 140
Speed Disk (SD), 2, 10, 37, 108-111,
  150
  aborting, 110
  ANSI-equivalent key combinations
    for, 14
  applications for, 109
  command-line options for, 108
  drive selection screen of, 109
  graphic display screen for, 110
  limitations of, 111
  problems while using, 110
  REPORT option for, 108
  using WIPEDISK with, 126
  WIPEFILE and WIPEDISK vs.,
    110
Speed Search, 10, 83, 85
  getting to Boot, FAT, and root
    directory areas using, 146

startup disks, 156, 157
string search, 118, 151
Sub-Directory menu, 25
subdirectories
  sorting of, 33
  too long list of, 150
SYSINFO.COM, 112
SYSTEM files, 12, 44, 47
  finding, 50
  using WIPEFILE with, 130
System Index (SI), 112, 113
System Information (SI), 11, 112-114,
  151
  applications for, 114
  command-line options and switches
    for, 112
  limitations of, 114
  TI Professional Computer report
    using, 113
  turbo clone report using, 114

T

task timing, 11, 115, 152
technical information, 11, 112
text files, printing of, 71, 152
text format, 144
Text Search (TS), 11, 118-120, 151
  command-line options for, 118
  hardware requirements of, 119
  recovering data using, 120
  translating EBCDIC to ASCII with,
    119
text-format display, 28
TEXTSRCH.COM, 118
time, 11, 115, 152
Time Mark ™, 11, 115-117, 152
  command-line options for, 115
  hardware requirements for, 116
TIMEMARK.COM, 115
TM.COM, 115
TM.EXE, 115
tone files, 8, 30, 152
  applications for, 31
  BEEP, 30
  creation of, 32
  duration, frequency, repetition, and
    pauses for, 30
  setting parameters for, 31
  translating sheet music to, 32
TREE utility, 79, 150
TREEINFO.NCD file, 78

Trojan Horse programs, 60, 62
troubleshooting, 149-158
TS.COM, 118
TS.EXE, 118
TYPE command, 71

U

UD.COM, 121
UD.EXE, 121
unfragmenting files, 66
UNREMDIR.COM, 121
UnRemove Directory (UD), 11, 121
  command-line options for, 121

V

VDISK.SYS utility, 7
VL.COM, 122
VL.EXE, 122
VOLABEL.COM, 122
Volume Label (VL), 11, 122-123, 152
  applications for, 122
  command-line options for, 122
  hard disk use of, 123
  valid volume names for, 123

W

wildcard characters, 9
windows, 137
WIPEDISK, 11, 12, 110, 124-128, 151
  command-line options for, 124
  FORMAT command and, 126, 127
  map disk screen display for, 127
  performance of, 125
  preventing cross-linked files with,
    126
  screen report from, 126
  using Speed Disk with, 126
WIPEDISK.COM, 124
WIPEDISK.EXE, 124
WIPEFILE, 11, 97, 110, 129-133, 151
  command-line options for, 129, 130
  explicit and wild-card file
    specifications for, 131
  switches used with, 132
WIPEFILE.COM, 129
WIPEFILE.EXE, 129
WN, 30
word processing, 9
  using Norton Utilities with, 157
working copies, 1-3

Edited by Stephen Moore